Sermons on the Parables

SERMONS ON THE PARABLES

HOWARD THURMAN

Edited with an Introduction by
David B. Gowler and Kipton E. Jensen

ORBIS BOOKS
Maryknoll, New York 10545

ORBIS BOOKS
Maryknoll, New York 10545

Fathers and Brothers
MARYKNOLL™

Founded in 1970, Orbis Books endeavors to publish works that enlighten the mind, nourish the spirit, and challenge the conscience. The publishing arm of the Maryknoll Fathers and Brothers, Orbis seeks to explore the global dimensions of the Christian faith and mission, to invite dialogue with diverse cultures and religious traditions, and to serve the cause of reconciliation and peace. The books published reflect the views of their authors and do not represent the official position of the Maryknoll Society. To learn more about Maryknoll and Orbis Books, please visit our website at www.maryknollsociety.org.

Texts by Howard Thurman copyright © 2018 by Anton H. Wong for the Thurman Family

Introduction and commentary copyright © 2018 by David B. Gowler and Kipton E. Jensen

Published by Orbis Books, Box 302, Maryknoll, NY 10545-0302.

Thanks to Friends United Press for permission to reprint "Concerning Prayer" (Chapter 15), previously published as "Prayer and Pressure" in Howard Thurman, The Growing Edge (Richmond, IN: Friends United Press, 1974), 45–53.

Excerpts from "Meditations of the Heart" by Howard Thurman
Copyright © 1953, 1981 by Anne Thurman
Reprinted by permission of Beacon Press, Boston

Queries regarding rights and permissions should be addressed to: Orbis Books, P.O. Box 302, Maryknoll, NY 10545-0302.

Manufactured in the United States of America

Library of Congress Cataloging-in-Publication Data

Names: Thurman, Howard, 1900-1981, author.
Title: Sermons on the Parables / Howard Thurman ; edited and introduced by David B. Gowler and Kipton E. Jensen.
Description: Maryknoll : Orbis Books, 2018. | Includes bibliographical references and index.
Identifiers: LCCN 2018004226 (print) | LCCN 2018019390 (ebook) | ISBN 9781608337491 (e-book) | ISBN 9781626982833 (pbk.)
Subjects: LCSH: Jesus Christ–Parables–Sermons.
Classification: LCC BT375.3 (ebook) | LCC BT375.3 .T48 2018 (print) | DDC 226.8/06–dc23
LC record available at https://lccn.loc.gov/2018004226

To our siblings,
Rick Gowler and Nancy Gowler
and
Kealei Castle and D. J. Jensen

CONTENTS

FOREWORD

We are a people. A people do not throw their geniuses away. And if they are thrown away, it is our
duty as artists and as witnesses for the future to collect them again for the sake of our children, and if
necessary, bone by bone.

—*In Search of Our Mothers' Gardens*, Alice Walker

Howard Thurman was a spiritual genius who transformed
persons who transformed history. Our journey into the future will be more promising if Thurman's contributions are
remembered, studied, and understood by current and coming generations. In *Parables of Jesus*, David B. Gowler and
Kipton E. Jensen have gifted us with a resource for remembering and re-membering (bone by bone) Howard Thurman. Their focus on Thurman's sermons about the parables
provides insights into essential elements of his spirituality.

The editors have transferred to the printed page sermons that previously had been available only on tapes or
compact disc recordings. *Parables of Jesus* is a more accessible medium for receiving and pondering Thurman's interpretations of the parables. When we hold this book in our
hands, we sit among the listening congregations as our
hearts and minds experience the parables through Thurman's heart and mind.

This collection of sermons makes evident sources of
authority that inform Thurman's spirituality. Obviously,
the scriptures are a fundamental source for his spiritual

wisdom and guidance. Thurman enters the scriptures with
the conviction that they have the power to deepen understanding of spiritual truth, moral meaning, and faithful
discipleship. The sermons focus on Jesus as the central authority for Christian faith. Jesus creates the parables that illumine what God is like, what God desires, and what God
desires of us. For Thurman, Jesus embodies the messages
of the parables. Jesus is teacher and exemplar. And even
more, the tone of Thurman's preaching indicates that he
is devoted to Jesus as his trustworthy companion.

These sermons portray not just Thurman's view that
scripture is an authoritative source for discerning Christian
discipleship but also his belief that life experiences and reason can be authoritative sources for spiritual discernment.
He repeatedly uses questions to direct listeners to examine
their motives and behaviors. This method bespeaks belief
in each person having a sense of self that is capable of dis-
covering ultimate meaning for living faithfully.

A vivid example of Thurman relying upon the power of
questions in personal examination (through reasoning,
prayer, and reflection) is evident in his sermon "The Prodigal Son." The sermon begins with a prayer in which Thurman asks seventeen questions to stimulate within all those
praying a "sense [of] some order in our lives, some specific
sense of direction, something that will tend to structure our
confusion so that we may understand its character."

Thurman's sermons challenge listeners to take seri-
ously the reality that their lives have ultimate significance.
They experience ultimate meaning and joy to the extent
that their lives align with God's will for creation. With all his
emphasis on being still and quiet, Thurman stresses that
the parables accentuate the need for an urgent response to
their spiritual truths. Becoming still and quiet have the in-
strumental function of enabling individuals to focus on
what is most meaningful. Such centering is not an escape
from relationships and social activism; it is the means to ex-

perience a transformed life that embraces relationships and activism.

We hear Thurman in these sermons insisting that individuals must take responsibility for their lives and for expressing compassion in community. The welfare of persons and community are inextricably linked. Choosing to attend to one while neglecting the other is not only folly, it fails to prepare for God's coming Realm.

I heard a preacher say, "Some people who have a problem with Jesus are actually resenting and resisting the persons who introduced them to Jesus." Over decades of presenting Howard Thurman's interpretation of Jesus, I have experienced many who felt that Thurman's portrayal of Jesus, to quote New Testament scholar Marcus Borg, was like "meeting Jesus again for the first time." Thurman introduced them to a Jesus who was in solidarity with the disinherited. A Jesus who stood against oppressive cultural mores and systemic injustice. A Jesus who did not demand adherence to a particular creed, but who did command followers to enact compassionate deeds. A Jesus who was an inspiration to contemporary struggles for freedom and shalom. In addition, Thurman's spiritually grounded and prophetic life as a follower of Jesus supported his interpretation of Jesus as trustworthy.

The first sermon of this book delivers a message of ultimate hope. Thurman says, "the contradictions of life are not final." What is nourishing and creative will come to fruition, just as what is depleting and destructive will fail. Fulfillment is experienced by living according to the will and creative energies of God. Whatever is meant by God's judgment and salvation (becoming whole) involves the conclusion that we have the choice to cast our lives with or against the ways of God's Realm. As we choose, we become aware that what God desires will prevail. This message on ultimate outcomes sets the stage for the dramas of our lives. Thurman's preaching insists that we are living the parables.

They are stories about the consequences of our life choices. Yes, living the parables is challenging; however, we live them with the assurance of hope.

This is the reassuring message of Martin Luther King, Jr. when he quotes Theodore Parker in saying, "The arc of the moral universe is long, but it bends toward justice." The message is also evident in Archbishop Desmond Tutu's declaration during the rule of South Africa's apartheid government that "apartheid is already dead." Injustice will not ultimately prevail. This book gives us not only an understanding of Howard Thurman's spirituality of the parables, it gives us a spirituality of hope for beloved community.

Geniuses enable us to perceive reality differently. Such new perceptions save us from indifference to what is true and beautiful and imaginable and possible. When we conclude that the gifts of these individuals enliven us to life, we celebrate them. However, when their genius threatens our sense of security with the familiar, they often face ridicule, censorship, prison, or even death. Perhaps the unforgivable response to geniuses is to throw them away by forgetting them and their contributions. Gowler and Jensen help us to remember (and re-member) the genius of Howard Thurman in ways that inform their own scholarly disciplines of New Testament and philosophy, as well as Thurman's genius for personal transformation and beloved community. *Parables of Jesus* provides insights about a spiritual genius whose life was committed to enacting the lessons of Jesus for his generation and generations to come. I believe these sermons inspire and empower us to go and do likewise.

Luther E. Smith, Jr., PhD
Author, *Howard Thurman: The Mystic as Prophet*

PREFACE

This book is a labor of love, one born out of convivial conversations between two scholars with very different areas of specialization: Kipton Jensen of Morehouse College is a philosopher. David B. Gowler of Emory University (Oxford College) is a New Testament scholar. Kipton was writing a book about the philosophical dimension of Howard Thurman's thought. David was writing a book about the use and impact (reception history) of the parables of Jesus in visual art, music, literature, theater, and other media over the centuries. During a series of informal conversations that included sharing various insights from these separate projects, Kipton suggested a joint venture in the area in which their interests intersected: a book on Howard Thurman's creative and significant interpretations of the parables of Jesus gleaned from a treasure trove of audios of Thurman's sermons, most of which had not yet been transcribed or published.

My [David] scholarly journey with Thurman stems from my work on the life and teachings of the historical Jesus. I have studied, taught, and written about the historical Jesus and his teachings for more than three decades—this is my third book on the parables of Jesus, for example—and have also deliberated over the relevance of Jesus's teachings for contemporary society. In brief, Jesus was a first-century apocalyptic prophet of Jewish restoration theology

and a prophet of social and economic justice for an oppressed people. His teachings in many ways represent a
"voice from below," a humane, commonsense approach of
a first-century Jewish non-elite person. As Thurman aptly
observes, historical Christianity is distinct from and, indeed, often greatly in contrast with the historical Jesus in
fundamental and troubling ways. In addition, I have ex-
plored how or even whether cultural and other assumptions from an ancient, advanced agrarian society can be
made relevant for understanding the will of God concerning questions facing people living in today's society. For
me, Thurman's *Jesus and the Disinherited* helps bridge the
gap between Jesus, the first-century peasant artisan Jew
from Galilee, and Christianity, the world religion that
claims to be based upon his life, message, and ministry.
Thurman reminds us that Jesus spoke primarily to those
who were oppressed by the powerful and that Jesus's
prophetic message continues to be relevant to the oppressed in any age and in every place, albeit in ways not
completely understood or acknowledged by many who
claim to follow him. Jesus of Nazareth, according to Luke
4:18–19, proclaimed good news to the poor, release to the
captives, and liberation of the oppressed. That message
can still resonate today, because it is still as relevant as
when Jesus first proclaimed it in the villages of Galilee. In
addition, I admire and agree with Thurman's contention
that an encounter with the teachings of Jesus—truly understanding his message—involves much more than just intellectual assent; understanding must lead to concrete action
in the world, because truly understanding Jesus's radical
message creates in us a profound moral obligation. Jesus's
teachings, including the parables discussed in this book,
not only *challenge* us to act; they *demand* that we act. Thurman's insights thus have been an inspiration to me, and
therefore I must also express my appreciation to Kipton for
his invitation to work on this book together and the ways in

which he has served as a reliable guide in my additional explorations in the life and work of Howard Thurman.

For me [Kipton], this edited collection of Thurman's sermons constitutes the culmination of a long inward journey, both personal and professional, since first reading *Jesus and the Disinherited*, which "hit me like a wallop," to use one of his many memorable phrases. I feel deeply indebted to Thurman for what he has taught me about myself and about what the religion of Jesus requires of us when it comes to caring for our neighbors. When I first encountered Thurman's writings, I could not have imagined that I would one fine day end up teaching—as I have been over the past seven years—at Thurman's beloved alma mater, Morehouse College. Thurman attracted me to Morehouse, where I sometimes teach in the same building where Thurman taught almost ninety years ago, but it is also Thurman who has brought me back to the bedrock faith of my childhood. My own experience is perhaps illustrative of how Thurman has provided, and continues to provide, for so many people a conscientious way back home to the religion of Jesus and the proverbial faith of our fathers.

It is sometimes said that the spiritual teacher we choose depends on the sort of person we are—and that certainly seems true of my own fascination with Thurman's thought—but it also seems true that the person we become depends on the teacher we choose. In choosing Thurman, I chose well. Thurman's winsome words and arresting images work their way into our heads as well as into our hearts.

I want to thank the late Vincent Harding, who was confidant to both Thurman and Martin Luther King Jr., for his encouragement in my early research into Thurman. I must also express my gratitude to those students and colleagues, especially Ms. Brenda Steele, who spent so many hours with me over the past years listening to Thurman's sermons in the Howard Thurman Listening Room on the third floor of Sale

Hall at Morehouse College. It was from each of them that I gained strength and courage to undertake this labor of love. Last but not least, I want to thank my co-editor, David, for his patience and insight as well as for his friendship.

After much reflection, we as editors decided to transcribe Thurman's sermons on the parables as he delivered them in the 1950s, with very little editing. We have preserved, for the most part, Thurman's exact words on the audios of these sermons and lectures. The advantage to this editorial light hand is that readers can better approximate the spirit in which Thurman delivered these sermons. Our task in this volume was to make available to readers Thurman's profound insights on the parables and his distinctive ways of communicating those insights. Even the inclusion of the occasional lapses in speech or the errors that he corrects, for example, helps to highlight the humanity of Thurman, his humor, and the deep connections he made with his audiences. We also realize, however, that, as with any source from decades ago, there are elements that are disconcerting if not offensive to modern readers. First among these outdated patterns of speech is the use of masculine nouns and pronouns instead of inclusive language. The decision not to change that language was a difficult one, but ultimately we agree with Luther Smith that Thurman's life and work bear witness to Thurman's belief in gender equality.[1] We therefore ask readers not only to remember that the most recent of Thurman's sermons included in this volume was preached by him more than sixty years ago but also to re-experience these sermons with that context in mind. Better yet, we hope that this book convinces readers that

---

1. Luther Smith Jr., *Howard Thurman: Essential Writings* (Maryknoll, NY: Orbis Books, 2010), 9. We discovered, after reading Smith's thoughts about Thurman's view on gender equality, that our own thoughts closely echoed those of Smith.

they should also listen to these and other sermons to gain an even greater appreciation of Howard Thurman.[2]

Thurman reminds us, gently, that "we are all of us indebted to a vast host by which we are surrounded." We want to thank the Thurman family, especially Anton Wong, for their sustained support and encouragement for this project. As one sign of our gratitude to Howard Thurman and his family, we will donate all royalties generated by this book to the Howard Thurman Educational Trust at Morehouse College. We also wish to acknowledge Pat Graham, Brandon Wason, and Bo Adams of Pitts Theological Library at Emory University, who made the Thurman audios available to us; the archivists of the Thurman Papers at the Gotlieb Center of Boston University, who provided transcripts of some of these sermons; the archivists at the Moorland Spingarn Research Center at Howard University; the Stuart A. Rose Library of Emory University for the image of Thurman that graces the cover of the book; Oxford College of Emory University, which generously supports David Gowler's scholarly activities; and the Morehouse College Archive and King Collection. In addition, we want to thank Luther Smith, who wrote the foreword to this volume and who paved the way for so many other Howard Thurman scholars through his own work.[3] We are also grateful to Robert Ellsberg at Orbis Books for his enthusiastic support of this project. The mission of Orbis Books, with its commitment to social justice, facilitating inclusive dialogues, and working for reconciliation and peace, makes it a perfect home for this volume.

Our brothers and sisters—Rick Gowler, Nancy Gowler, Kealei Castle, and D. J. Jensen—to whom we have dedicated

---

2. See www.morehouse.edu/thurman/sermons.

3. See, for example, in addition to Smith, *Essential Writings*, his book, *Howard Thurman: The Mystic as Prophet* (Richmond, IN: Friends United Press, 1992).

this book, continue to inspire us with their spiritual commitment and deep hunger for God, and they also bring to
mind all of those whom Thurman described as our "unknown and undiscovered brothers and sisters" for whom
this book is meant as well.

As we write these words on Christmas Day, 2017, we conclude with one of our favorite Howard Thurman poems,
"Now the Work of Christmas Begins." This poem succinctly
describes our responsibility to participate actively in the
work that began after "the song of the angels" ended and
continues until there is "music in the heart" of all people:

> When the song of the angels is stilled,
> when the star in the sky is gone,
> when the kings and princes are home,
> when the shepherds are back with their flocks,
> the work of Christmas begins:
> to find the lost,
> to heal the broken,
> to feed the hungry,
> to release the prisoner,
> to rebuild the nations,
> to bring peace among the people,
> to make music in the heart.[4]

David B. Gowler
Oxford College of Emory University

Kipton E. Jensen
Morehouse College

---

4. Howard Thurman, *The Mood of Christmas and Other Celebrations*
(Richmond, IN: Friends United Press, 1985), 23.

INTRODUCTION

Howard Thurman (1899-1981)
"Tutor to the World"

It is difficult to identify precisely the influences that shape and fashion the life of an individual. The enigma is the process at work in the private world of an individual that finds its expression in the thoughts, words, and actions that ultimately emerge. It has been aptly said that the time and place of a man's life is the time and place of his body, but the meaning and significance of a man's life is as creative, as vast, and as far-reaching as his gifts, his dreams, and his response to his times can make them.[1]

The Howard Washington Thurman National Memorial, an obelisk dedicated to Dr. Howard Thurman, the 1923 valedictorian of Morehouse College, stands on the Morehouse campus in Atlanta, Georgia. Inside the obelisk—engraved in black marble and near the burial niche where the ashes of Howard and his wife Sue Bailey Thurman are interred— there is a quote from Sue Bailey Thurman that describes

---

1. This quote comes from Thurman's introduction in Olive Schreiner, *A Track to the Water's Edge: The Olive Schreiner Reader*, edited by Howard Thurman (New York: Harper & Row, 1973), xviii–xix.

her husband as a "seeker and finder of genuine existence
—a tutor to the world." These words, for those unfamiliar
with Howard Thurman's work and legacy, may seem audacious if not presumptuous. The obelisk itself, in fact,
stands in the plaza just outside the Martin Luther King Jr.
International Chapel. This chapel, dedicated to the memory of Dr. King, an even more famous Morehouse alumnus,
overshadows—in the annals of history and memory—the
memorial to Thurman. But just as one must pass by the
Thurman Memorial physically on the Morehouse campus
to enter the front door of the King International Chapel,
one cannot understand King's theology and philosophy
without first understanding Thurman's.

Howard Thurman played a vital role in laying the spiritual foundation—not only by providing the arguments but
also by setting the religious tone and the spiritual accent—
for the early civil rights movement in the United States. Yet
Thurman's importance goes well beyond his influence on
King and others in the civil rights movement. His legacy
stands on its own, and his spiritual gifts and dreams, as well
as his unique response to his troubled times, were as ex-
traordinarily creative as they were vast and far-reaching.[2]

HOWARD THURMAN'S LIFE AND CAREER

In his autobiography, *With Head and Heart*, published when
he was seventy-five, Thurman observed that he could describe only the "highlights of a career because it is impossi-

---

2. A foundational element of Thurman's convictions is the fact
that Thurman really did believe that Jesus "was on the side of freedom, liberty, and justice for all people, black, white, red yellow, saint,
sinner, rich, or poor." Howard Thurman, *With Head and Heart: The
Autobiography of Howard Thurman* (New York: Harcourt Brace Jovanovich, 1979), 114.

ble to describe a life."[3] Thurman's career, however, could
well be viewed as a series of bold adventures that woven together constitute a noble if not divine quest in search of
common ground and dynamic integration, both within and
without, with head and heart, and attempts to approximate
the beloved community.

Thurman was born in West Palm Beach and raised in
Daytona, Florida, by Saul Solomon Thurman and Alice Ambrose Thurman. Thurman was just seven when his father
died, and he was crushed when the itinerant preacher used
his father's funeral as an occasion to delineate the fire and
brimstone that await those who "died outside of Christ."
Thurman then and there vowed that he would never become a minister of the church. And although Thurman was
ordained twenty years later, he always resented how that
churchman in Daytona had "condemned [his] dead father
and so grievously traumatized [his] young life."[4]

Thurman said that his maternal grandmother, Lady
Nancy Ambrose, a slave in northern Florida during her
youth, a midwife and the hub of the church community in
Daytona, was the person who taught him more about the
genius of the religion of Jesus than any of his other teachers or later professors. Grandma Ambrose instilled in her
three children and all her grandchildren the fact that they
were in no way slaves, nor were they second-class citizens:
"They were God's children!"[5]

Thurman was most at home near the water's edge,
along the banks of the Halifax River or on the beaches of
the Atlantic Ocean. He felt a natural kinship with all living

---

3. Thurman, *Head and Heart*, xiii.

4. Ibid., 261; Thurman describes his father's funeral on pages
5–6. In the summer of 1917, Thurman's older sister Henrietta died of
typhoid fever at the age of twenty. Thurman was seventeen.

5. Ibid., 21.

things, seeking the face of God, for example, beneath his favorite oak tree in Daytona. In such settings, Thurman "prayed to God and talked with Jesus,"[6] and he conversed with Jesus in his mind throughout his life, always asking himself anew what Jesus might have said and done in this or that particular situation.

At home, Thurman found refuge and consolation in his mother's arms. In 1910, as Halley's comet was flying overhead, Thurman asked his mother what would happen if the comet crashed. She offered comfort and reassurance, whispering to him as he fell asleep: "God is going to take care of us."[7]

Thurman always was an exceptionally bright student, but his educational opportunities were limited because of his race. Since there was neither a middle school nor a high school open to African Americans in Daytona, Thurman attended high school at Florida Baptist Academy, about 110 miles away in Jacksonville, Florida, where he often worked nights to pay for his room and board. In 1918, despite many obstacles, Thurman graduated from the Academy as valedictorian.

Thurman then received a scholarship to attend Morehouse College, a black liberal arts college for men in Atlanta, Georgia. In that city, just as in St. Augustine, Thurman was constantly confronted with the looming threat of racial violence. He lived through what many historians have called the nadir of race relations in the post–Civil War United States, when Jim Crow laws and extra-legal forms of intimidation and violence ruled the South. The year Thurman enrolled in Morehouse is known as the "Red Summer" of 1919 because of race riots in more than three dozen cities, including Houston, St. Louis,

---

6. Ibid., 266.
7. Ibid., 15.

Chicago, Omaha, Tulsa, and Charleston. Thurman writes tersely of this period in Georgia's history: "Lynchings, burnings, unspeakable cruelties were the fundamentals of existence for black people."[8] Within the relatively safe confines of the Morehouse campus, however, Thurman grew by leaps and bounds. A voracious reader, Thurman was an economics major with a concentration in religion. In addition, his mathematics professor, Dr. Benjamin E. Mays, who would later become the president of Morehouse, whetted Thurman's lifelong passion for philosophy.

Thurman graduated as valedictorian of Morehouse College in 1923. As Mark Giles aptly notes:

The earning of a college degree in 1923 placed Thurman in a small but growing group of Blacks earning college degrees in America and stood in critical contrast to what many other Southern Blacks experienced that year. For example, 1923 was also the year of the Rosewood, Florida massacre. The opportunity for Blacks to attend school and college and contribute to their communities during this time period should be understood within the context of Jim Crow America."[9]

Thurman confessed that the racism he suffered in his youth "left its scars deep in my spirit and has rendered me terribly sensitive to the churning abyss separating white from black."[10] But Thurman's fate, he would have said, was not his destiny. Although the time and place in which

---

8. Ibid., 36.

9. Mark Giles, "Howard Thurman: The Making of a Morehouse Man, 1919–1923," *Journal of Educational Foundations* 20, no. 1–2 (2006): 106.

10. Howard Thurman, *The Luminous Darkness* (New York: Harper & Row, 1965), 10.

Thurman lived was shot through with racism and poverty as well as imperialism and militarism, he always perceived the good as well as the bad.

From Morehouse Thurman traveled to Rochester Theological Seminary, now Colgate Rochester Crozer Divinity School, which at that time accepted only one or two African American students each academic year. Thurman was an exceptional seminarian in terms of the ambition of his academic work, his church service, and his numerous off-campus speaking engagements. Rochester also provided Thurman's first sustained and intimate encounter with the white world. It was there that he began to extend what he called his "magnetic field of awareness to other than my own people."[11] Racism was less overt in Rochester than in Atlanta, but toward the end of his years in Rochester, for example, Thurman met a man who said that he had "heard practically every sermon you have preached since last fall" and that the Klan had carefully recorded "where [Thurman] went, what [his] subjects were, and how many people were in [his] audience."[12] Thurman, as a Black academic and theologian, often faced expectations to address issues of racial injustice, but there were also cautionary voices urging him to avoid such controversies. One of Thurman's favorite professors at Rochester Theological Seminary, for example, advised him that "it would be a terrible waste for [Thurman] to limit [his] creative energy to the solution of the race problem, however insistent its nature" and that he should give himself instead "to the timeless issues of the human spirit." Thurman admits that he struggled to find an adequate response "to this man who did not know that a man and his black skin must face the timeless issues of the human spirit together," and he sought throughout his life to

---

11. Thurman, *Head and Heart*, 51.
12. Ibid., 50.

"grow more and more rich in knowledge and in all manner of insight" so he could effectively address this question and other fundamental issues of human existence.[13] Thurman married Katie Kelley in 1926 and almost immediately began his work as pastor of Mount Zion Baptist Church in Oberlin, Ohio. He was by all accounts a wonderful pastor from the very beginning, and he notes that it was as a "pastor that [he] learned that the human spirit is capable of great nobility."[14] Katie was already suffering from an illness that she had contracted during her years of social work, and, because of Katie's worsening health, the couple with their young daughter, Olive, moved to Atlanta in 1928, where Thurman taught religion at Morehouse College and Spelman College and served as the director of religious life at both institutions. Thurman excelled as a teacher, both inside and outside the classroom, and he made a lasting impression upon his students. Benjamin Mays, sixth president of Morehouse (1940–1967), described Thurman's impact on his students in this way: "When they heard or read him, for the first time they experienced a free man and his freedom was contagious."[15]

During 1929, Thurman studied mysticism with Rufus Jones at Haverford College, and Jones remained a significant influence in Thurman's own work. After Katie died of tuberculosis in 1930, a grieving Thurman traveled to Europe and sought to "recover his center," to search deep within himself, to rediscover the essence of who he was, and, in doing so, to reconnect with God his Father. As in his childhood, the ocean was once again cathartic for Thurman; it

---

13. Ibid., 60.

14. Ibid., 71.

15. Benjamin E. Mays, *Debate and Understanding: Simmering on the Calm Presence and Profound Wisdom of Howard Thurman* (Boston: Martin Luther King, Jr., Center for Career, Educational and Counseling Services at Boston University, 1982), 86.

was one of many places that permitted him to engage in the long stretches of silence that his inner life required and to keep "alive the flickering flame of the spirit when the harsh winds blew and the oil was low in the vessel."[16]

In 1932, Thurman married Sue Bailey, and the couple moved to Washington, DC, where Thurman taught in the School of Religion at Howard University and subsequently served as dean of Rankin Chapel. In 1935, Thurman was selected as the chairman of the "Negro Delegation" on a Pilgrimage of Friendship to India sponsored by the World Student Christian Movement; both Howard Thurman and Sue Bailey Thurman traveled throughout India as well as Ceylon (now Sri Lanka) and Burma (now Myanmar) for almost a year. Thurman writes in his autobiography about a number of eye-opening experiences on the journey, but two events stand out. First, in what turned out to be the most momentous human encounter on their trip, the Thurmans met with Mahatma Gandhi in 1936. Thurman was sympathetic to Gandhi's doctrine of nonviolence, ahimsa, prior to their meeting in Bardoli, and it was easy to draw analogies between the plight of the colonized masses in India or "coloreds" in South Africa and the dire straits of Blacks in America, especially in the South.[17] At the end of their lengthy and

---

16. Thurman, *Head and Heart*, 17.

17. There is a tradition of African American pacifism that stretches back at least as far as Benjamin Banneker (1731–1806), who advocated directly or indirectly for religious and philosophical pacifism, disuse of oaths, and the abolition or reduction of the death penalty. Like Thurman, and perhaps in part because of him, Martin Luther King Jr. was convinced that the religion of Jesus combined with the nonviolent resistance philosophy of Gandhi "was the only morally and practically sound method open to oppressed people in their struggle for freedom." See Martin Luther King Jr., "My Pilgrimage to Nonviolence," *Fellowship* 24 (1958): 9.

spirited discussion, Gandhi asked the Thurmans to sing the great African American spiritual, "Were you there when they crucified my Lord?" This hymn, thought Gandhi, got to "the root of the experience of the entire human race under the spread of the healing wings of suffering."[18]

Thurman's second key experience in India occurred early one morning at the Khyber Pass, now part of Pakistan. In brief, Thurman had an epiphany as he observed the sun rise over Kinchinjunga; it was a watershed experience for Thurman which, "at its core, confirmed the possibility of true human community." As he noted:

> All that we had seen and felt in India came miracu-lously into focus: *we knew that we must test whether a religious fellowship could be developed in America that was capable of cutting across all racial barriers, with a carry-over into the common life, a fellowship that would alter the behavior patterns of those involved. It became im-perative, now, to find out if experiences of spiritual unity among people could be more compelling than the experi-ences that divide them* [italics ours].[19]

One effect of Thurman's sojourn in India can be seen in how, after his return to Howard University, he described his ministry as "an exploration of the problems that arise in the experience of people who attempt to be Christian in a society that is essentially un-Christian."[20] Followers of the religion of Jesus, he insisted, were "those who were willing to exercise the limit of power and moral suasion upon

---

18. Thurman, *Head and Heart*, 134.

19. Howard Thurman, *Footprints of a Dream: The Story of the Church for the Fellowship of All Peoples* (New York: Harper & Brothers, 1959), 24.

20. Walter Earl Fluker et al., eds., *The Papers of Howard Washington Thurman*, vol. 2 (Columbia: University of South Carolina, 2012), xix.

men in the interest of the redemption of themselves and society" and who could "against the darkness of the age see the illumined finger of God guiding in the way they should go."[21] Whether in religious or academic institutions, Thurman decried what he perceived to be a "preening other-worldliness" and "a callow materialism." The "apocalyptic heritage of the black church," as he put it, "left it ill-equipped to deal with either the spiritual or practical realms of existence."[22] When one of his Howard University colleagues in the Sociology Department argued that what African Americans really needed was to "enrich themselves and learn to speak the language of economic power and control," Thurman objected that the religion of material-ism was "soul-killing" and, no less than racism and materi-alism, was rooted in fear, deception, and hatred. Whatever distorted or warped the personality, whatever injured or killed the soul, whether segregation and poverty or impe-rialism and militarism, was for Thurman "not only unethi-cal" (though it was clearly unethical or immoral for those very reasons), it was also "a mortal sin against God." Thur-man believed that "the view that the traditional attitude of the religion of black people was, or is, otherworldly is su-perficial and misguided," because it "gave the member a fontal sense of worth that could not be destroyed by any of life's outrages."[23]

Although he already had tenure at Howard University, and while he was gaining national renown as a preacher

---

21. Howard Thurman, *Deep Is the Hunger: Meditations for Apostles of Sensitiveness* (New York: Harper & Brothers, 1951), 5.

22. Howard Thurman, "Higher Education and Religion," in *Papers of Howard Washington Thurman*, vol. 1 (2009), 121; also see Quinton Dixie and Peter Eisenstadt, *Visions of a Better World* (Boston: Beacon Press, 2012), 46-48.

23. Thurman, *Head and Heart*, 17–18.

and teacher, in 1944 Thurman and his family accepted an offer to move to San Francisco to become co-pastor of an interfaith and interracial church: The Church for the Fellowship of All Peoples. This was the opportunity to which Thurman sought to put his Khyber Pass epiphany to the test.

Moving into his new pastoral role, Thurman was primarily concerned with a "deepening of the spiritual life" of those who gathered together for worship. In the midst of a diverse intercultural, interracial, interfaith, and interdenominational community of faith, Thurman declared that "the one thing we had in common was a vast hunger for a better way of living together than we had ever known and a deeper spiritual hunger that only the God of life could satisfy."[24] The "basic discovery" that surfaced at the Fellowship Church, one that confirmed Thurman's earlier intimations, was that "meaningful experiences of unity among peoples were more compelling than all that divided and separated."[25] If what Thurman accomplished in San Francisco could be replicated elsewhere, and if it could be sustained for a sufficient duration of time and at an quantifiable degree of intensity, he thought, then just maybe a qualitative socio-spiritual transformation could occur such that:

> together a way could be found to lift the burden of war and the threat of war from the heart, to move the great weight of poverty from the backs of the poor, to bring in a time a tranquility when everywhere, at home and abroad, the barriers that separate shall be no more and men will love and

---

24. Ibid., 143.
25. Ibid., 148.

trust each other and nations will dwell together as friendly peoples underneath a friendly sky.[26]

Barriers were already crumbling, slowly but surely, it seemed; the divisions were disintegrating; and the boundaries that had previously prevailed were steadily giving way.

During his time in San Francisco, Thurman's fame and influence continued to grow. In 1953, for example, *Life Magazine* hailed Thurman as one of the twelve "Great Preachers" in the United States, "the country's most eminent preachers ...shaping the spiritual life of America..."[27] Also in 1953, at about the time when Martin Luther King Jr. was finishing his coursework in the School of Theology at Boston University,[28] Thurman joined Boston University's faculty and administration as the dean of Marsh Chapel and as a professor of spiritual resources and disciplines. The invitation to serve as dean of Marsh Chapel was unique, audacious, and historically significant, because Thurman was the first African American to serve in such a position at a predom-

---

26. Ibid., 210.

27. *Life Magazine* (April 6, 1953): 126-32. In 1954, *Ebony Magazine* called Thurman one of the ten best Black preachers in the United States, saying he was "Polished, poetic, and some say, hypnotic in the pulpit...His ideal is to erase all barriers between God and man, and between man and man. Dr. Thurman gives a church service some of the atmosphere of a concert hall." "Great Negro Preachers," *Ebony* 9, no. 9 (July 1954): 2–30. Cf. Thurman, *Head and Heart*, 171. See also Lerone Bennett, "Howard Thurman: 20th Century Holy Man," *Ebony* 33, no. 4 (February 1978): 68–85.

28. Thurman and King, in fact, watched the 1953 World Series together, perhaps rooting for the Brooklyn Dodgers, who had ended racial segregation of major league baseball by adding Jackie Robinson to their roster in 1947. The Dodgers lost to the New York Yankees in six games, although the Dodgers won their World Series rematch against the Yankees in 1955.

inantly white university.[29] In his later years in Boston, Thurman traveled extensively as minister-at-large, and, in 1963, Thurman finally made it to Africa, where he taught in Nigeria. In 1965, Thurman and Sue Bailey Thurman returned with much fanfare to San Francisco, where Thurman directed the Howard Thurman Educational Trust until his death in 1981. The mission of the Thurman Trust was to provide college scholarships for Black students, especially in the South, and to disseminate Thurman's writings as well as audio and video recordings.[30]

HOWARD THURMAN AND THE CIVIL RIGHTS MOVEMENT

Thurman sought novel ways of restoring wholeness to the hearts and minds of individuals within religious or spiritual communities. The manifold contradictions of life, he insisted, would not have the last word. While it may be true that Thurman's teachings are timeless yet always timely, it is also true that his writings and sermons serve as a lens through which to reexamine the role of religion in the early civil rights movement, especially since Thurman claimed that "the test of any religion, as far as its impact upon mankind is concerned, turns on what word does it have to share about God with men who are the disinherited, the

---

29. Many educational institutions were still segregated in 1953, since it was only on May 17, 1954, that the U.S. Supreme Court issued its Brown vs. Board of Education ruling, which declared that segregated public educational institutions were unconstitutional.

30. One of the fruits of that effort is this book of Thurman's sermons on the parables, which we have collected from the archives of Boston University and Emory University, two institutions that received gifts of numerous audios, videos, and documents of Howard Thurman from the Thurman family.

outsiders, the fringe dwellers removed from the citadels of power and control in the society."[31]

Although he was not at the frontlines of political activism, Thurman did attend the March on Washington in 1963. Otis Moss, himself an unsung hero of the civil rights movement, suggests that while Thurman "did not march from Selma to Montgomery, or many of the other marches, [he] participated at the level that shapes the philosophy that creates the march—and without that, people don't know what to do before the march, while they march, or after they march."[32] Although Thurman said that he "never considered himself as any kind of leader" nor "a movement man," Albert Raboteau reminds us that one of Thurman's chief insights was that "true social change must be grounded in spiritual experience and personal transformation."[33]

Thurman wrote in 1966 about the sort of dynamic integration, as opposed to what he called token integration, that he considered necessary to reconfigure and recover from the damage done to both body and spirit by segregation. Though he had witnessed so much cruelty, Thurman still seemed to believe that we were capable of redemption, individually and collectively, and that "community cannot feed for long on itself; it can only flourish where always the boundaries are giving way to the coming of others from beyond them—unknown and undiscovered brothers."[34]

---

31. Thurman, *Luminous Darkness*, xi.

32. Bennett, "Howard Thurman," 71.

33. Albert Raboteau, "In Search of Common Ground: Howard Thurman and Religious Community," in *Meaning and Modernity: Religion, Polity, and Self,* edited by Richard Madsen, William M. Sullivan, Ann Swidler, and Stephen M. Tipton (Oakland, CA: University of California Press, 2002), 158.

34. Howard Thurman, *The Search of Common Ground: An Inquiry into the Basis of Man's Experience of Community* (New York: Harper & Row, 1971), 104.

Thurman was one of the first in a long line of African American intellectuals to meet with Mahatma Gandhi in India. When Thurman asked Gandhi what had adulterated the message of nonviolence in India, Gandhi replied that it was the Hindu caste doctrine and the treatment of untouchables. What puzzled Gandhi was why American Christianity was seemingly impotent to transform the social and economic conditions for minorities in America and, second, why slaves and descendants of slaves in the United States did not convert in greater numbers to Islam, since—said Gandhi—"the Moslem religion is the only religion in the world in which no lines are drawn from within the religious fellowship."[35] Thurman thought that the history of slavery and segregation in America, analogous to the plight of the untouchables in India, undermined the vitality of the institution of Christianity and, in fact, was a betrayal of the faith of Jesus. Thurman's response was to appropriate and adeptly apply the philosophy of nonviolence to the problem of racism as well as to materialism and imperialism in America. This perspective was founded on Thurman's own understanding of Jesus of Nazareth, an understanding that sought to restore Christianity as a religion of the weak and oppressed, not a religion—as Christianity too often had become—of the rich or otherwise powerful who conspired to exploit other human beings.[36] The result of this cross-fertilization was a distinctively African American philosophy of nonviolent but active resistance to social injustice.

Although today he is perhaps best known, if known at all, as a mentor to Martin Luther King Jr., Thurman's thoughts and words were repeatedly put to the test during

---

35. Thurman, *Head and Heart*, 132.

36. Howard Thurman, *Jesus and the Disinherited* (Boston: Beacon, 1996), 20. Originally published by Abingdon Press in 1949.

the civil rights movement. At the first meeting of the Southern Negro Leaders Conference, later called the Southern Christian Leadership Conference (SCLC), in 1957, Bayard Rustin asked King, "Do you remember what Gandhi told Howard Thurman in India, many years ago?" He then recited Gandhi's seemingly prophetic words that "it may be through the Negroes that the unadulterated message of nonviolence will be delivered to the world."[37] In many ways, that prophecy proved true. As Luther Smith notes, "the development of a philosophy of nonviolent protest for the black struggle is a foremost achievement of [Thurman's] social witness."[38]

Thurman's sermons and writings provided succor and sustenance to an entire generation of civil and human rights activists. Lerone Bennett claims that when he "went to Montgomery, shortly after the beginning of the bus boycott, [he] was not at all surprised to find King not reading Gandhi but Howard Thurman."[39] According to Bennett and Andrew Young, King carried a copy of Thurman's *Jesus and the Disinherited* with him almost everywhere he went.[40] Congressman John Lewis says that he and the other freedom riders from across the country circulated Thurman's writings, especially *Deep River* (1945) and *The Negro Spiritual Speaks of Life and Death* (1947), as a source of spiritual courage at a time when they were asked to do the impossible.[41] Thurman was—and still is—pertinent to each one of us, and he becomes something special to each person in

---

37. Dixie and Eisenstadt, *Visions of a Better World*, 45.

38. Luther E. Smith Jr., *Howard Thurman: The Mystic as Prophet* (Richmond, IN: Friends United Press, 1992), 133.

39. George K. Makechnie, *Howard Thurman: His Enduring Dream* (Boston: Howard Thurman Center, Boston University, 1988), 39.

40. Bennett, "Howard Thurman," 68–85.

41. From a personal conversation with Representative John Lewis.

our own way. Thurman strove throughout his life to melt away the persistent if not pernicious obstacles or barriers and differences that divide us from our undiscovered brothers and sisters.

THURMAN AND THE HISTORICAL JESUS

The historical Jesus is essential to Thurman's understanding of religious experience and, in his view, the religion of Jesus is the true essence of Christian theology. The religious experience of Jesus is a paradigmatic example of a radical encountering of God's loving presence and a commitment to a transformative personal relationship with God (and, as a result, with other human beings). In addition, Jesus was a member of an oppressed group, a "disinherited" person speaking to other disinherited people who, like Jesus, had their "backs against the wall." Jesus's life and teachings sought to empower the disinherited and help them gain a sense of community (the kingdom of God), and an essential element of Jesus's message was speaking prophetic words against the oppressors of his people.[42] The life and message of Jesus thus is foundational to the transformation of individual human beings and the transformation of society. As Thurman observes about Jesus: "Wherever his spirit appears, the oppressed gather fresh courage; for he announced the good news that fear, hypocrisy, and hatred, the three hounds of hell that track the trail of the disinherited, need have no dominion over them."[43]

---

42. Thurman, *Jesus and the Disinherited.* See also Smith, *Howard Thurman*, 108–9.

43. Thurman, *Jesus and the Disinherited*, 29.

Thurman was a devout Christian and an ardent defender of the faith, but he entreats us to reconsider the sociopolitical situation and historical context within which Jesus—"this wonderful person," as he calls him in the first sermon in this collection[44]—taught us with respect to overcoming the triple evils of fear, hatred, and deception by means of radical, dangerously unselfish love.

Thurman insists that the person, life, and teachings of Jesus provide crucial insights for all human existence. Through Jesus, for example, God identifies with and empowers the disinherited. As Luther Smith notes, for Thurman:

> Jesus is Christianity's exemplar because of the way he (being fully human) was able to reveal God's truth within and about the human condition. This was a truth which affirmed justice and righteousness, the dignity of all people, the necessity for love to rule all relationships, and the power of love to overcome evil and create community.[45]

By the time he met Gandhi (1936), Thurman delicately distinguished the religion of Jesus from the conspicuous injustices that are historically inseparable from the institution of Christianity, whether by omission or commission, whether exercised abroad or at home. During his visit to Colombo, Sri Lanka, in 1935, for example, Thurman was asked how he could represent Christianity to the people of Sri Lanka and India after his "forebears" had been enslaved by Christians in America and, even after having been liberated from slavery, had been brutalized, lynched, and de-

---

44. Chapter 1, "Growth and the Kingdom of God."
45. Smith, *Mystic as Prophet*, 109.

nied basic civil rights by those who claimed to be Christians. Thurman's answer to this question is indicative of his approach to Jesus, the Bible, Christianity, religion, and the evils in society:

> It is far from my purpose to symbolize anyone or anything. I think the religion of Jesus in its true genius offers me a promising way to work through the conflicts of a disordered world. I make a careful distinction between Christianity and the religion of Jesus. My judgment about slavery and racial prejudice relative to Christianity is far more devastating than yours could ever be. From my investigation and study, the religion of Jesus projected a creative solution to the pressing problems of survival for the minority of which He was a part in the Greco-Roman world. When Christianity became an imperial and world religion, it marched under banners other than that of the teacher and prophet of Galilee. Finally, the minority in my country that is concerned about and dedicated to experiencing that spirit that was in Jesus Christ is on the side of freedom, liberty, and justice for all people, black, white, red, yellow, saint, sinner, rich, or poor.[46]

These insights about the religion of Jesus were developed more fully in *Jesus and the Disinherited*, but Thurman's understanding of the parables of Jesus is critical to his understanding of the relationships between God, Jesus, and humanity.

---

46. Thurman, *Head and Heart*, 113–14.

THURMAN'S SERMONS ON THE PARABLES OF JESUS

Thurman was one of the very finest and most influential preachers of his day. Although he also published numerous books and articles, "[his] craft remained the spoken word,"[47] and this collection comprises a spectrum of sermons or soliloquies and meditations of sundry sorts of Thurman's "spoken words" on the parables of Jesus. Without wanting to suggest that the sermons we have selected for this volume are unique or even "essential," we consider these sermons on the parables of Jesus to be seminal and representative as well as suggestive of new frontiers of Thurman scholarship.

Thurman's interpretations of Jesus's parables should be seen in light of his spiritual prescription of a centering process that oscillates according to a principle of alteration between centripetal meditation, the inward pull, and centrifugal movement, the outward concern, as the working out of our collective salvation and the divine purpose for each and every person: "I am not myself alone, but I am a part of all the life that breathes through me and through which I breathe. We are all of us indebted to a vast host by which we are surrounded."[48] Thurman tries to provide his listeners with an atmosphere or environment within which participants are invited to center down within themselves and then come up refreshed in their resolve for their brothers here and their sisters there. When it comes to his interpretation of the parables, then, Thurman claimed that he was not "talking about the metaphysics of it or the philosophy of it—that's way up here—but I'm talking about the way you live, how you deal

---

47. Ibid., 227.
48. Chapter 1, "Growth and the Kingdom of God."

with your fellows, how you deal with yourself, how you move into the warp and woof of your daily experiences."[49] Indeed, Thurman's life could be construed as a sermon, and the entire corpus of his thought life and his writings could be aptly characterized as parabolic from start to finish. One of the finer functions of parabolic preaching in the Black Church is that it invites us, each in our own way, to change our lives and become less of "what we have become"—whenever we, like the prodigal son, wander off from God—and increasingly more of who we really are—whenever we, also like the prodigal son, return to our Father. In addition, Thurman argues, when we come to our Father, we also come to ourselves.[50]

Thurman thus believed that Jesus's parables provide crucial clues for "living in the present with dignity and creativity,"[51] and Thurman's interpretations of the parables in these sermons often surprise us—as do the parables themselves—in their utter simplicity and depth of insight.

For those readers already familiar with Thurman, this is not surprising. Lerone Bennett, for example, went so far as to describe Thurman as "one of the greatest minds of our generation" and "perhaps the greatest storyteller in the world."[52] For some, Thurman's voice was tantamount to hearing the voice of God Almighty; for others, Thurman quite simply exuded an authenticity that was both disarming and delightful. Some have suggested, as does Thurman himself, that a sermon should facilitate a collective mystical experience.[53] Thurman writes that in his ser-

---

49. Ibid.

50. See the discussion of the parable of the Prodigal Son in chapter 3.

51. Thurman, *Jesus and the Disinherited*, 11.

52. Bennett, "Howard Thurman," 70.

53. Mozella Mitchell describes Thurman as a technician if not a

mons and other acts of corporate worship, he always sought in earnest for "the moment when God appeared in the head, heart, and soul of the worshiper," which he considered the "moment above all moments, intimate, personal, private, yet shared, miraculously, with the whole human family in celebration."[54] Thurman asks us to recall, for example, that in the end this is between us, each of us, and God, as he observes in his sermon, "Growth and the Kingdom of God":

> the process of growth and development and unfolding is an inscrutable process. What does that mean? As touching the kingdom of God, the only thing that I am responsible for doing...is to not block the process. That I lay bare my mind and will and heart to what seems to me to be the truth of God, and that I follow the light that I have.[55]

For many of his listeners, it wasn't so much the message, or even the words, but more the tone, the intonation, the pauses, the gestures, and, for some, it was the sheer expression on his face—animated by sincere puzzlement or insight. In listening to audio recordings of his sermons, one senses that even Thurman's pauses are pregnant with meaning. He himself notes that the written sermons "reveal aspects of my own pilgrimage without benefit of the magic

---

shaman of the sacred who did "not simply bring the message of truth from God to the religious community, but he leads individuals and the community to have an experience of the divine from which they may gain a sense of wholeness themselves": *Spiritual Dynamics of Howard Thurman's Theology* (Bristol, IN: Wyndham Hall, 1985), 88.

54. Thurman, *Head and Heart,* 159; also see Thurman, *Deep Is the Hunger,* 24.

55. Chapter 1, "Growth and the Kingdom of God."

of the spoken word, the creative pause, and the lifted countenance."[56] For many of those who heard Thurman preach, the overarching impression was one of real intimacy, a warmth of climate and personality, authenticity, an inspiring degree of integrity—both in the ethical sense and in the sense of wholeness—the opposite of the disintegrated individual, as well as a sense of the sacred, of someone "stripped bare of all pretense and false pride,"[57] to use a phrase from Thurman, and utterly exposed or otherwise vulnerable and receptive to the spirit of God.

Thurman's correspondence makes clear, however, that he was sometimes dissatisfied with his liturgical experiments in fostering an atmosphere of worship. What Thurman delivered, more or less extemporaneously, demonstrated his own understanding of the immediacy of the experience, his openness to the movement of the spirit, the freshness of it all. By some accounts, both in the classroom and chapel, he seemed to be thinking it through—entreating us to "think with him for a minute"—with his companions and congregants. One gets the sense that it was more than rhetorical flourish when Thurman said, as he often did in his sermons, "What do you think about that?" This searching together for answers, of struggling to "untie the knot" of these thought-provoking parables, as Søren Kierkegaard describes it,[58] is inherent in the nature of Jesus's parables. The parables are often puzzling in their tendency to take up residency in one's head and heart; they both enlarge the heart and stimulate the imagination, as do Thurman's

---

56. Howard Thurman, *The Growing Edge* (New York: Harper & Brothers, 1956), x.

57. Thurman, *Jesus and the Disinherited*, 103.

58. Søren Kierkegaard, *Training in Christianity* (New York: Vintage Books, 2004), 117–18.

sermons and reflections on the parables. Indeed, Thurman is at his best when explicating Jesus's parables as "can-openers for the mind" (see chapter 1, "Growth and the Kingdom of God") that creatively serve as aids to self-examination, self-knowledge, self-surrender, self-overcoming, and self-determination. Thurman knows that we not only interpret parables but that parables also, in many ways, interpret us.

Conclusion

At a baccalaureate address at Spelman College, Thurman said: "There is in you something that waits and listens for the sound of the genuine in yourself. Nobody like you has ever been born and no one like you will ever be born again—you are the only one. And if you miss the sound of the genuine in you, you will be a cripple all the rest of your life."[59]

Thurman's voice, whether written or spoken, expresses "the sound of the genuine," and two examples of what he eloquently said of others could aptly be applied also to him. First, Thurman spoke out of the depths of his own center and his own Christian religious tradition, and part of the eulogy he gave for Martin Luther King Jr. describes Thurman as well: "Always he spoke from within the context of his religious experience, giving voice to an ethical insight which sprang out of his profound brooding over the meaning of his Judeo-Christian heritage" and he was "able to put at the center of his own personal religious experience a searching ethical awareness."[60] Second, Thurman's message extends

---

59. Howard Thurman, "The Sound of the Genuine," *Spelman Messenger* 96, no. 4 (Summer 1980): 14–15.

60. Thurman, *Head and Heart*, 223.

far beyond what he would consider the artificial boundaries of Christianity as it is (mis)understood today to address issues universal to the human condition in a way reminiscent of how he described Rabindranath Tagore, the Hindu poet-mystic: "His tremendous spiritual insight created a mood unique among the voices of the world. He moved deep into the heart of his own spiritual idiom and came up inside all peoples, cultures, and all faiths."[61]

Although it is important to rehearse the times and places of his life, it is even more important to recognize that there is something about Howard Thurman's thought that is timeless yet always timely. Thurman provides vital resources for our present times. We seem to need him now as much as—if not more than—ever.

---

61. Ibid., 129.

A Chronology of Thurman's Life and Career

1899   Thurman is born in West Palm Beach and raised in Daytona, Florida, by Saul Solomon Thurman and Alice Ambrose.

1918   Thurman graduates as valedictorian from high school in St. Augustine, Florida.

1923   Thurman graduates as valedictorian at Morehouse College.

1925   Thurman is ordained as a Baptist minister.

1926   Thurman graduates as valedictorian at Rochester Theological Seminary (later Colgate Rochester Crozer Divinity School), which typically accepted only one African American student each academic year. Marries Katie Kelley and becomes pastor of Mount Zion Baptist Church in Oberlin, Ohio.

1927   The Thurmans' daughter, Olive, is born.

1928   Because of Katie's tuberculosis, the Thurman family moves from Ohio to Georgia, where Thurman teaches religion at Morehouse College and Spelman College as well as serving as the director of religious life at both institutions. Katie and Olive spend part of their time with the Kelley family in La Grange, Georgia.

1929   Thurman studies mysticism with Rufus Jones at
         Haverford College.

1930   Katie Kelley-Thurman dies.

1931   Thurman travels extensively in Europe.

1932   Thurman marries Sue Bailey, and the couple
         moves to Washington DC, where Thurman
         teaches in the School of Religion and
         subsequently serves as dean of Rankin Chapel
         at Howard University.

1933   The Thurmans' daughter, Anne, is born.

1935/6   Howard Thurman and Sue Bailey Thurman travel
         to India as well as Ceylon (now Sri Lanka) and
         Burma (now Myanmar) on a preaching tour;
         Thurman serves as chairman of the "Negro
         Delegation" on a Pilgrimage of Friendship spon-
         sored by the World Student Christian Movement.
         Howard and Sue meet with Mahatma Gandhi in
         1936.

1944   Thurman accepts the position of co-pastor of an
         interfaith and interracial church in San Francisco,
         The Church for the Fellowship of All Peoples.

         The Greatest of These is published.

1945   *Deep River* is published.

1947   *The Negro Spiritual Speaks of Life and Death* and
         Meditations for Apostles of Sensitiveness are
         published.

1949   *Jesus and the Disinherited* is published.

1951   *Deep is the Hunger: Meditations for Apostles of Sensitiveness* is published.

1953   Thurman accepts a position as dean of Marsh Chapel—as well as professor of spiritual resources and disciplines—at Boston University.

Meditations of the Heart is published.

1954   *The Creative Encounter* is published.

1956   *The Growing Edge* is published.

1957   "Apostles of Sensitiveness" (The Ware Lecture) is published.

1959   *Footprints of a Dream* is published.

1960   Thurman takes a trip around the world, spending time primarily in Pacific Asia.

1961   *Mysticism and the Experience of Love* and *The Inward Journey: Meditations on the Spiritual Quest* are published.

1962   *Temptations of Jesus* is published.

1963   Thurman travels to Africa, spending time primarily in Nigeria.

Disciplines of the Spirit is published.

1965   Thurman and Sue Bailey Thurman return to San Francisco, where Thurman directs the Howard Thurman Educational Trust.

The Luminous Darkness: A Personal Interpretation of the Anatomy of Segregation and the Ground of Hope is published.

1969   *The Centering Moment* is published.

1971   *The Search for Common Ground: An Inquiry into the Basis of Man's Experience of Community* is published.

1973   *The Mood of Christmas* is published.

1979   *With Head and Heart: The Autobiography of Howard Thurman* is published.

1981   Thurman dies on April 10.

GROWTH AND THE KINGDOM OF GOD

The Sower (Mark 4:1-9)
and the Seed Growing Secretly (Mark 4:26-29)

Thurman begins this 1951 sermon series on the parables of Jesus (chapters 1-7 in this book) by discussing how parables have always challenged the hearts, minds, and imaginations of their hearers and readers ever since Jesus first spoke them. Thurman's comment that Jesus's parables "stimulate the mind," for example, echoes the famous definition of parable by C. H. Dodd:

A parable is a metaphor or simile drawn from nature or common life which grabs the listener by its vividness or strangeness and which leaves sufficient doubt about its precise application so that it teases the mind into active thought.[1]

The ambiguity, the open-endedness, the polyvalence of Jesus's parables functions as a key aspect of their power to impact their hearers and readers.

This sermon also illustrates Thurman's awareness of contemporary debates in parable scholarship, such as what materials in the Jesus traditions actually stem from Jesus and what materials stem instead from "the minds who have preserved for us the records." In addition, Thurman's

---

1. C. H. Dodd, *Parables of the Kingdom*, rev. ed. (Glasgow: Collins, 1961), 16.

observation that the references to the "kingdom of God" in Jesus's teachings have been "stripped of [their] political significance" needs to be evaluated in the larger context of Thurman's discussions in his classic work, Jesus and the Disinherited. In that light, interpreters should realize that some parables, just like other teachings of Jesus, contain his radical critiques of the elites who oppressed those "with their backs against the wall." Although those people at or near the bottom rungs of society in first-century Palestine in both economic and political terms could not really function in "politics" as we define it today, prophets such as Jesus of Nazareth courageously proclaimed God's judgment against the powerful elite in strong terms. Jesus, in that sense, was extremely "political," which is the primary reason he ended up dying on a Roman cross.[2]

Jesus, as a first-century Jewish peasant-artisan—like others "with their backs against the wall"—often used what James C. Scott calls "the weapons of the weak" to resist their oppressors in ways that seem ambiguous.[3] The example Thurman cites of Jesus "steadfastly" seeking "to keep himself separate from political involvements" could also be seen as a tactic of ambiguity typical in peasant resistance to overwhelming power and oppression: Jesus's answer is so ambiguous that it is difficult to accuse him of treason against Caesar, although it contains an implicit critique of the Roman Empire.[4]

This sermon focuses on the message about the kingdom of God as found in four "growth" parables: the sower, the seed growing secretly, the wheat and the tares, and the barren fig tree. We learn much about Jesus's view of the king-

---

2. Cf. Douglas E. Oakman, The Political Aims of Jesus (Minneapolis, MN: Fortress, 2012).

3. See James C. Scott, Weapons of the Weak: Everyday Forms of Peasant Resistance (New Haven, CT: Yale University Press, 1987), 175.

4. Since the denarius has the emperor's image on it (Luke 20:24), Jesus's words could be interpreted as saying, "Give that (blasphemous) coin back to that (blasphemous) emperor." Cf. Gerd Theissen, The Shadow of the Galilean (Minneapolis, MN: Fortress, 1987), 157.

dom" of God from these growth parables.[5] As Thurman observes, for example, in the parable of the seed growing secretly the growth of the seeds is independent of the effort of the sower, except for his planting good seeds properly in the ground. Likewise, the kingdom of God arrives independently of human efforts. Thurman thus also ponders how much human activity can either help bring about or hinder the coming of God's kingdom. Here Jesus's use of agricultural metaphors may also be informative. Jesus often uses nature in his parables to illustrate the kingdom of God because nature follows a predetermined and predictable cycle: sowers sow, crops appear, and the harvest follows. The implication in Jesus's message about the kingdom is that the same inevitability applies: God's kingdom will surely arrive (cf. where Thurman says, "it's bound by certain laws").

But Thurman assures us in this sermon that we do have a responsibility to work for and to nurture the growth of God's kingdom. Just as farmers are responsible for doing all they can to bring about and increase the growth of the fields they have planted—whether by preparing the soil, planting the proper seeds, irrigating the ground if needed—Christians also are responsible for doing all they humanly can to prepare for the coming of the kingdom of God.

Thurman's use of the wheat and tares parable is also interesting in several respects. He demonstrates his awareness of first-century contexts—tares could be poisonous, for example.[6] He also is aware of the ways in which this parable has been interpreted through the centuries. Is the parable speaking about wheat and tares in the church alone or wheat and

---

5. Jesus's Gospel teachings about the kingdom of God, as Thurman notes, alternately speak of the kingdom of God as a present reality and also as something that will come dramatically (or quietly) in the future.

6. As one of Thurman's favorite books on the parables notes, "Darnel is false wheat, hard to distinguish from real grain, and poisonous to eat." George A. Buttrick, *The Parables of Jesus* (New York: Richard R. Smith, 1930), 63. The Moffat translation and a number of other translations use the term "weeds" instead of "tares."

tares in the church and in the larger society![7] *Thurman instead opts for an even more difficult and challenging possibility: that the wheat and the tares are intermixed within human beings, that human beings are mixtures of both good (wheat) and evil (tares).*[8] *This interpretation, though, does not provide us with "an escape hatch," Thurman argues, that absolves us from the responsibility of being actively involved in creating a better society. All are responsible in the world of parable and in the world in which we live.*

To give us some hope that our efforts will not be futile, Thurman turns to Jesus's numerous images of the certain harvest that awaits us: There will be a final resolution between good and evil, and Thurman believes that Jesus is thereby suggesting that our universe "ultimately does not sustain tares" (evil), because this universe, this world, and the human beings living in it are all God's. Therefore we should work assiduously to be on God's side and to do our best to help bring about God's positive and creative harvest.

GROWTH AND THE KINGDOM OF GOD

September 2, 1951

MEDITATION AND PRAYER

[We] gather together in the quietness. Each one seeking the level of his own resting place, each one reaching out for

---

7. Perhaps most famously reflected in the debates about religious liberty between Roger Williams and John Cotton, where Williams argued that neither the church nor the state should use any coercive force against perceived heretics. See David B. Gowler, *The Parables after Jesus* (Grand Rapids, MI: Baker Academic, 2017), 147–51.

8. A view Thurman shares with such interpreters of the parable as varied as Macrina the Younger and Flannery O'Connor. See Gowler, *Parables after Jesus*, 45, 218–23.

peace of mind and spirit in terms that he can understand and in ways that are meaningful. Crowding around the quietness of the many-tongued voices of the traffic of our lives. The restlessness of our age, the churning tumult of our times, the quiet frustrations and the riotous frustrations in the midst of which we live and the temple of which we have somehow committed to our hearts and minds. All these surround us in the quietness, and yet we recognize the privilege of unhurried contemplation, of laying ourselves bare to the searching processes of singleness of mind, the privilege of becoming aware of needs of which we are scarcely conscious in our fevered rush, the privilege of hearing voices that need not speak above a whisper in our hearts, pointing us to the way that we should take in the midst of our own problems and responsibilities, our own hopes, and our own fears. The time of quiet. The time of searching of heart. The time of regaining of perspective. The time of lifting of hopes about ourselves and the world. The time of insight. The time of the renewal of courage.

O God, our Father, we thank thee for the quiet time and for all that it says to the weary, to the proud, to the self-righteous, to the fearful, to the human spirit. Accept our thanks, O God, our Father. Amen.

SERMON

[Mark 4:1–9: The Sower][9]
Once more he proceeded to teach by the seaside, and a huge crowd gathered round him, so he entered a boat on the sea and sat down, while all the crowd stayed on shore. He gave them many lessons

---

9. The New Testament readings in this sermon mostly follow the Moffatt Bible translation. See James Moffatt, *A New Translation of the Bible* (New York: Harper & Brothers, 1954).

in parables, and said to them in the course of his teaching: "Listen, a sower went out to sow, and as he sowed it chanced that some seed fell on the road, and the birds came and ate it up; some other seed fell on stony soil where it had not much earth, and it shot up at once because it had no depth of earth, but when the sun rose it got scorched and withered away, because it had no root; some other seed fell among thorns, and the thorns sprang up and choked it, so it bore no crop; some other seed fell on good soil and bore a crop that sprang up and grew, yielding at the rate of thirty, sixty, and a hundredfold." And then he added, "Anyone who has ears to hear, let him listen."

[Mark 4:26–29: Seed Growing Secretly]
[And Jesus said,] "It is with the kingdom of God as when a man has sown seed on earth; he sleeps at night and rises by day, and the seed sprouts and shoots up; he knows not how. For the earth bears crops by itself, the blade first, the ear of corn next, and then the grain full in the ear. But whenever the crop is ready, he has the sickle put in at once, as harvest has come."

[Matthew 13:24–30: Wheat and Weeds]
"The kingdom of heaven [Jesus said] is like a man who sowed good seed in his field, but while men slept his enemy came and re-sowed weeds among the wheat and then went away. When the blade sprouted and formed the kernel, then the weeds appeared as well. So the servants of the owner went to him and said, 'Did you not sow good seed in your field, sir? How then does it contain weeds?' He said to them, 'An enemy has done this.' The servants

said to him, 'Then would you like us to go and gather them?' 'No,' [he said,] 'for you might root up the wheat when you are gathering the weeds. Let them both grow side by side till harvest; and at harvest-time I will tell the reapers to gather the weeds first and tie them in bundles to be burnt, but to collect the wheat in my barns.'"

[Luke 13:6–9: Barren Fig Tree]
[And he told this parable.] "A man had a fig tree planted in his vineyard; he came in search of fruit on it but he found none. So he said to the vine-dresser, 'Here have I come for three years in search of fruit on this fig tree without finding any; cut it down, why should it take up space?' But the man replied, 'Leave it for this year, sir, till I dig round about it and put in manure. Then it may bear fruit next year. If not, you can cut down.'"

I want to think with you for a few mornings very directly and simply about the insights of the parables—certain of the parables at any rate—the parables, the whole idea of parables, of telling a tale to illustrate a moral. [The parable] is, I suppose, as old as human speech. Certainly it was not created by Jesus. It was a part of his heritage, and he used it very effectively and very simply. The parables have always excited the imagination of men, because they have tried to see all sorts of things in them, and it's a wonderful thing to do with your mind, you know, to read one of these and then start playing with it, to see what this means and that means and the other means, and of course you know quite directly that Jesus didn't have that in mind, but you may say, "Well, I don't know what he had in mind exactly; it's pretty obvious in one or two places, but at any rate, it's a good clothesline on which I can hang my particular garment." And that's all

right, because it acts as a can opener for the mind, you
know—well, that's not a good figure [laughter], but it's...
Well, you understand what I mean: It stimulates the mind.

The parables about which we are thinking this morning, the parables of growth, have to do with the kingdom of
God. And it is very interesting that when Jesus thought
about the kingdom of God, it *seems* as if he stripped it of its
political significance. I don't know whether he actually did
it or whether the minds who have preserved for us the
records have given it that angle. For the kingdom of God in
Israel meant that which was fundamentally political as well
as righteous, as moral. When Israel dreamed of the coming
of the kingdom of God, it was a time when the powers that
were in control of the political and economic and social life
that had created so many circling series of embarrassments
and torture and misery for Israel would be destroyed, and
the political, social, economic, religious power of Israel
would be restored, for Israel regarded itself as not only [a]
religion, but a culture and a civilization as well.

But when Jesus thinks about the kingdom, certainly in
the records that we have, it is something which seems to be
devoid of the political ramification. He steadfastly sought
to keep himself separate from political involvements. Now,
whether that was due to the kind of critical environment in
which he functioned, and he did not want to precipitate
something that would cut off the fulfillment of his ideas, I
don't know—but when they wanted to make him a king, he
refused; when they said, "This tribute, is it lawful to pay tribute to Caesar?" he said, "Pay to Caesar that which belongs
to Caesar and to God that which belongs to God."

It's very puzzling, but the kingdom of God in [Jesus's]
thought, at any rate, has to do with a quality of life under
the rule and the domination of God. Now what is that kingdom like? Is the kingdom coming? Sometimes Jesus seems
to say, "Well, the kingdom is at hand," and sometimes he

seems to say that the kingdom is already here. Sometimes he suggests that the kingdom will come in with great noise, with great stirring, and then at other times that the kingdom will come silently. The kingdom is in the world, and the kingdom is in the heart. No man knows when it will come, and every man stands in candidacy for its coming, for whatever a man is who has the rule of God in his heart, there the kingdom of God is at hand. It's very interesting the way Jesus's mind and spirit seem to grapple with the paradoxes inherent in the concept itself.

So these three parables, four that I read to you, have to do with his treatment of the kingdom, his idea about how the kingdom will come. [In] one of them, he says that the kingdom of God is like unto a man who planted his field, and then he went to bed. He slept, and he got up the next day and worked. The next night he went to bed and slept. Then after many days, the harvest was ready. The kingdom of God comes independent of human effort aside from the initial act.

It's very interesting. Let's think about that. The growth of the seeds that the farmer planted is independent of the farmer's thought, hopes, actions, except having good seed and planting it properly, obeying the fundamental proposition that's involved in the seed/dirt relationship. Once that has been obeyed, then there isn't any more that can be done, that the mystery that surrounds the swelling of the kernel and the bursting open and the releasing of the elemental vitality that is transformed in terms of shoots and leaves and the rest of it. All of that is an act of God. That there isn't anything I can do about it.

It's very interesting. That the process of growth and development and unfolding is an inscrutable process. What does that mean? As [to] the kingdom of God, the only thing that I am responsible for doing, [Jesus] seems to suggest, is to be sure that to the limit of my power I do the elemental cooperation: I see that I do not block the process. That I lay bare my mind and will and heart to what seems to me to be the truth of God, and that I follow the light that I have. I don't know. What do you *think* of that? What do *you* think of that?

It's very interesting to me how this idea has dogged the footsteps of man. There is always a sense in which it seems as if the human spirit can do nothing. When you really think about it, how much can you do? How much can you do about anything? That's not a very healthy idea, but how much can you do? How much can do you? How much power do you have? Can you make your hair grow? Despite what is going on in the funny paper [laughter], the comic strip about the man who's working on that idea. Can you make yourself short or tall? Can you by willing it do this or that? Or is this the kind of universe [where] somehow you can garner up enough of pure desire and great singleness of mind, that you can hold that desire and singleness of mind at dead center until at last the most stubborn and un-yielding aspects of your life or the life of the world will take the objective shape of your inward desire?

Is that the kind of world this is? Or, even when that happens, are you ever sure that you do any of it? This is an interesting Gospel—I see that I am taking all the time on this one, but I don't mean to. It is a very interesting Gospel because, you see, in times of great, great futility in human life, in times when all of the social processes are bankrupt, then this idea becomes a very important haven of refuge. And I confess to you that as I have been reflecting upon this all week and then thinking about what's happening in San Francisco this week and what happened yesterday, this kind of funny treaty that we've signed that puts all the resources of America to back a lily-white Australia and New Zealand.[10]

---

10. Thurman is referring to the Australia, New Zealand, and United States Security Treaty (ANZUS Treaty) that was signed in San Francisco on September 1, 1951.

As I began to think about all this, I said, "Well now, why should I worry about that? This is God's world, and God will do it." But I don't know. Maybe I have to do something. But you see, it's a comforting thing to take refuge in. When German civilization collapsed after the first World War, it was very easy for certain German theologians to develop a concept that the kingdom of God is a mystery that only God understands and that God will superimpose upon the traffic of life, that there isn't anything that anybody can do about it, so I can only wait and trust and hope that he will make up his mind to move in time to spare my life, but if he doesn't, then I can only say he had other plans.

The kingdom of God is like a seed that is planted by a farmer, and he plants it and knows that he is responsible for doing all that his power permits, bringing to bear upon the selection of his seed as much wisdom and intelligence and farmer sense as he is able to garner, to understand the nature of the seed as fully as possible and what kind of soil the seed needs and prepare that soil. And after he has exhausted all of his resources in that particular, to cooperate with the relentless logic of the process of growth. Then relax and have no bad dreams. You've done all you can do. But the curious thing is you are never sure! [laughter] Never sure.

The second aspect of growth in one of the other parables is a man planted his field. He did everything that he should do, and then found that mixed up with this good wheat there were tares, there were things that were not wheat. And the tares in this period, what is described here, tares [are] seen by authorities to be something that looked like wheat but wasn't wheat, and if you ate it, it killed you; while if you ate wheat, you didn't die as soon [laughter].[11]

---

11. Tares might be bearded darnel; it can kill livestock and even people, if it is eaten.

Now, when the attendant saw these curious things growing up in the midst of the wheat, he said, "But didn't you plant all wheat?" It's very interesting that Jesus introduces that little phrase in there. He gave the planter of the wheat the benefit of the doubt.

> [Attendant]: "Now think back, before you blame the universe, before you blame somebody, think back: Did you do it?"

> [The planter]: "Well, if you put it that way, yes, I did. I remember now. It's all back in my mind. I did this and this and this. Yes, all the wheat was good."

> [Attendant]: "Well, how do you account for this?"

> [The planter]: "An enemy did it. An enemy! I didn't."

> [Attendant]: "Now, can I pull it all up then, pull all these tares out?"

> [The planter]: "No, you can't do it that way."

And this is very interesting. I'm always intrigued by the insight that Jesus shows here.

> [The planter]: "You can't do it that way, because this is the kind of universe in which the wheat and the tares grow like that. And if you start pulling out every tare, you'll destroy the wheat."

And I'm always tempted to apply that to society, you see, as one more escape hatch for me so that I won't be required to do anything, you see. And you may take delight in feeling self-righteous, with reference to that same idea.

Now, it is very hard for me to apply it to myself. How the wheat and the tares are mixed up inside of *me*. What a mixture of good and evil am I! Over and over again, here is a great, deeply moving, profoundly significant ethical insight that seems to be distilled out of purity of heart and great zealousness with reference to the purposes of God. And by the time it gets where it's going, it's so mixed up and confused that it does, when it finally lands, it does what at the time I didn't know that I had in mind. Whenever I see it I have the sneaking suspicion that maybe that was a part of my intent. It's a terrifying thing: wheat and tares.

And then I want to get the tares pulled out, when I get a fresh insight, and then in my quietness and in my meditation I lay bare all of my substance before God. And in the discerning of his eye, I see reflected the meaning of this and this, so that under his scrutiny, I recognize that this is tare and this is wheat. And I'm so emotionally stirred by what I see, so convicted of my error and my sin, that I want to tear up the whole business, clean it out. And then I discover that the quality of my very being is involved in wheat and tares.

Now there is a profound presupposition [of] Jesus in this parable to which I feel I must call your attention. That even though growth is a process, it is invisible, it's involved in the vitalism of life, yet it's bound by certain laws: There is a time of reaping, and when the reaping time comes, then you know the difference between the wheat and the tares. This note of judgment that seems always creeping through all the thinking of Jesus: that ultimately the mind and the spirit cannot find peace and rest in a final dualism, if the wheat and the tares forever and ever are that way. Then you have a world in which there is always a persistent struggle between good and evil, and that struggle is an infinite, ultimate struggle, with no solution. Therefore, if that is the position, you see, that's this end of the wheat and the tares, you see, there they are, that's the way life is.

Now if the contradictions of life are ultimate contradictions, if the contradictions of life are final contradictions, then there can be no hope of resolution! Do you see? Do you understand that? If the wheat and the tares are permanently characteristic of existence, then there can be no escape from the wheat and tare involvement. No final resolution. For it says, you see, that inherently and fundamentally, the quality of goodness and the quality of that which is not goodness are equally matched. That the bias that the human spirit seems to have on the side of the positive as over against the negative is an illusion. Now that's what it seems to suggest if, you see, there is no resolution.

But there creeps always into the thought of Jesus a very interesting thing, and you see it here in this parable. There shall be a harvest time, a harvest time. And when the harvest time comes, what happens? Then the true character of the wheat is revealed, and the true character of the tares is revealed, and the thing that he is suggesting is that this is the kind of universe that ultimately does not sustain tares. Do you believe that?

Now your options are very few. Very few. For you see...your conviction—not what you talk about, not what you really profess with your lips, but [the] thing that informs the quality of your living—is in sync (if I may put it that way) with one or the other of these two positions. You either are deeply convinced, you see, that this is the kind of universe in which the contradictions of life are final contradictions, and you know, then, if that is your position, you see. And you don't have to take that intellectually. I'm not talking about the metaphysics of it or the philosophy of it—that's way up there—but I'm talking about the way you live, how you deal with your fellows, how you deal with yourself, how you move into the warp and woof of your daily experiencing. It is the shadow that your life casts, the accent, the odor of your life, the aroma, the whole quality, the overtones; that's what I'm getting at. That is in sync with one or the other of these positions. For you see, if you're convinced that ultimately these contradictions are final contradictions, you'll know that you can't do anything, finally, about anything. That your life is a battleground between these two elemental, eternally equally-matched forces, one generating that which seems to be negative and destructive and the other generating that which seems to be positive and creative. And your little spirit is just a battleground for these, and so you decide that I know that my deeds can't affect anything beyond my little life, so for the days that I have, for reasons that are peculiar to me or for reasons that have to do with my own sense of decency, my own self-respect, my own positive answer to the negations of existence, for whatever may be the reasons, I may say that for my own little life, I will let the weight of my days count on the positive side of the contradiction rather than the negative side. I know ultimately it makes no difference, but I'll count on that side. And I do it, and in doing it, all the help that I can expect is a limited help, because goodness has the same hard job in the universe that it has in me. So maybe I can help it out a little by not putting my weight on the wrong side.

But Jesus did not seem to suggest that that is a sound position, for, you see, he insists that this is God's world, that this is God's order, God's universe, and that ultimately the contradictions of life are not final. There shall come a time, how soon I do not know, when the bias of my spirit that is on the side of that which is positive and creative will find a response that confirms and sustains it. [Jesus] calls it the harvest. Some other places he calls it the Great Judgment. He has all these phrases, but it means that *he* is insisting that the mind cannot find peace either in a contradiction or a paradox. So, I don't know how it will be resolved, but I do know, says Jesus, that harvest is inevitable, and when harvest comes, that which is wheat will still be wheat, and that which is tare will be tare. And stripped to the literal substance of each self, the tare is poisonous and deadly and destructive, and the wheat is sustaining. And I shall live my life on the assumption that that which is native to the structure of life and the universe is that which is inherently significant in the wheat. And because I believe that, I shall abide.

What do you think? How do you live it? And it is no answer at all to say that you haven't thought about it, because every day of your life you cast your vote. You cast *your* vote. On which side? Which?

2

SALVATION:
WHAT IS GOD LIKE?

The Lost Sheep and Lost Coin
(Luke 15:4-10)

"Everybody in some sense is lost."

George A. Buttrick's Parables of Jesus *seems to have inspired some of Thurman's musings in this sermon about the parables of the lost sheep and the lost coin. Buttrick, for example, discusses these two parables together before examining the parable of the prodigal son in a separate section;[1] likewise Thurman discusses the lost sheep and lost coin in this sermon—the second in his seven-sermon series on the parables—before treating the prodigal son in the next (chapter 3 below). In addition to gleaning details from Buttrick about first-century life reflected in these stories—such as how in the parable of the lost coin the only way for light to enter a house was usually through a door—Buttrick also asks the key question that interests Thurman in this sermon and, indeed, for most of his life: "What is God like?"*

As in several of the sermons about the parables in this volume, Thurman notes that the lost coin parable is a

---

1. George A. Buttrick, *The Parables of Jesus* (New York: Richard R. Smith, 1930), 176–86.

"very simple story,"[2] but one that has profound implications about the nature of God, the nature of human beings,
and the nature of the relationship between God and
human beings. Thurman envisions God working, for example, in the ways Thurman saw "modern society" (in 1951)
"finding the lost," such as modern medicine's "ministry of
healing." Thurman does not overemphasize that message,
but he does see all such "holy work" as part of God's redemptive process and argues that we should recognize God's
hand even in such apparently secular processes.

   Thurman notes that in the parable of the lost sheep
Jesus portrays God as a shepherd who loves and actively
seeks out the sheep who is lost. For Thurman, this portrayal
of the shepherd and the sheep also demonstrates the importance of community. The sheep was out of touch "with the
group that sustained him." A sense of isolation can occur
with human beings who wish to be "independent," and it
also can happen with nations—and have devastating results.
The parable teaches that, like the shepherd, God is not pas-
sively waiting; God takes the initiative and is always actively seeking and searching for those who are lost. What
the shepherd does for the sheep, God wants to do for
human beings: restore them to fellowship and the community in which they truly belong.

THE LOST SHEEP AND LOST COIN

September 16, 1951

MEDITATION AND PRAYER

[missing]...that break the heart and torment the mind.
But we are also bound together by the overtones of joy, by

---

2. As does Buttrick, *The Parables of Jesus*, 183.

all of the subtle reassurances of the daily round by which
our spirits are lifted and our confidence in life restored and
reestablished. The quietness, the stillness that permits the
sediment to gather and the clarity of our movement to be
defined. How dependent we are upon the hush, the great
silent movements of the Spirit.

O God, our Father, thou who art not far from any one
of us. How rich is the assurance that thou dost give to us.
And how desperate is our need for that assurance. May thy
Spirit that is in us—and that sometimes in these quiet
stretches seems so terribly near—may it brood over and
within all the peoples of the earth this day, those that are
now being broken by war, those that have been broken by
war, those that are now being broken by strength, those
that have been broken by victory. How dependent are we,
O God, upon thee, and how glad we are that it is so. Amen.

SERMON

For those of you who are seated where the sun casts its rays,
you have my sympathy [laughter], but we have not had sunshine for a long time, and I hope you ... [missing].

... have been most definitive is a point at which Christianity deals with the crucial question for all religions, and
that is the question of salvation. Everybody's interested in
salvation, whether you are a theologian or not. Everybody
wants to be saved, because everybody in some sense is lost.
When Jesus talked about salvation, he told three stories,
three parables, and you are very familiar with them, but I
suggest that when I talk to you about them, recapping them,
as it were, that you don't let your mind play hooky, saying
you know what I'm going to say about that, because you
don't [laughter].

These parables really have as much to do [with] salvation
as they have to do with the other most persistent question of

the human mind and human spirit, and that is, "What is God like? What is God like?" The earliest question that I remember raising as a little boy was, "Who made God? Where did God come from?" It worried me all the time, because I couldn't ever get any answer that was satisfying. And, of course, I don't have one now, because it is a question the answer to which one lives into, and the more deeply one lives into the answer, the more irrelevant becomes the question. It's interesting, but true, I think.

The first story had to do with a lady who had lost some money. A very familiar story. She lost a coin, and she looked everywhere for the coin—but, of course, the place where it was, until finally, she looked at that place, and there she found it. She had to light a candle, doubtless, because her house was dark. [There was] only one point at which light came into those houses, and that was through the door. And the shaft of light coming through the door could not get into the more involved parts of the house. So she looked everywhere, and when she found the coin, she did a very interesting thing: she told her neighbors, called her neighbors in, because, no doubt, she had told them that she'd lost it. You can be sure of that, because it's easier to tell about the negative thing than about the positive thing. That is also very interesting, but I won't go down that way.

So she said, "Come and rejoice with me, because I've found that which was lost, my coin, and now I'm very happy." Very simple story. A piece of money lost. "What is God like?" asks Jesus. He's like a lady who found a coin that had been lost, and the coin had been restored to its place of usefulness.

Very simple. Now let's look at it for just a minute or two before we go to the other. A coin lost through no act of its own. It couldn't think; it couldn't feel; it had no freedom of movement or motion except that [by] which it was propelled, for it was a thing. But, nevertheless, it was lost, and in that sense it was completely victimized by environmental factors and forces over which it had no control. Lost from one's meaning, because one is a victim of circumstances over which one has no control, but the result of which cannot escape one's responsibility. It's a curious thing, isn't it? Curious.

An accident at birth, and the whole structure of fulfillment along the lines that were potentially inherent in this throbbing body that was born. Bad teaching that focused the thought and the attention and the dynamics of the personality along channels of increasing error: lost, victim of circumstances.

Now, the list is long, and your list is as good as mine, and you can draw on your own experience in which you are thus involved. Now the interesting thing to point out in connection with the meaning of salvation in this parable is that being found meant the restoration of meaning within the limitations of the coin itself. To me one of the most sobering aspects of modern life is the way in which—and perhaps I'm prejudiced because of my own calling and vocation—but the way in which modern society—I want to say this with measured meaning—the way in which modern society, inspired, I think, by the Spirit of God, is at work in finding the lost who are lost because of the operation of impersonal factors and forces over which they have no control. And I think that the ministry of healing through all of the uses to which forces of nature are put in response to the creative wooing and urgencies of the mind of man and the desperation of his spirit, all of these are part of the redemptive process by which the God of the lost is seeking his own. All of the things that we do to help in the rehabilitation of children, all the things that we are working on in helping to restructure and helping to release creative forces that can restructure disturbances of the mind and the emotions—all of these are part of the redeeming process of God! And I think that the work is holy, and those who with their training and their minds are vehicles for that kind of redemption should be men and women of great reverence and great spiritual discernment and awareness. And the illusion that these processes are secular processes, the illusion that these processes are so objective, so scientific that they are not involved in the deeply moving spiritual thing with which life is instinct is perhaps the most tragic delusion of modern man.

What can happen when one with discipline and long-brooding with the mind and exposure to the need can have that whole process illumined by a recognition that God is at work in him. Every hospital, every clinic, every consultation, consulting room becomes an altar where the love of God burns for the redemption of his children.

And then the second, and I'll just touch it, perhaps... There was a sheep. It may have been a lamb, I don't remember, but let us say a sheep, because it fits better. A sheep was enjoying his grass and the other things that sheep enjoy as he went along, and then when he started feeling chilly, he didn't recall, but the only thing that he remembers is that suddenly he became aware that he was cold, and there was a throwback in his mind, and he realized that he had been cold for some time. But, the grass was good. Then he looked around, and he discovered that he was alone. That everybody had gone. That is, that all the sheep had gone. And he began crying aloud.

And then the shepherd, who had many sheep, missed him when he got back to the fold, and he left his ninety and nine—or whatever the number was—and he went out to try to find this sheep that was lost. And Jesus says, "God is like that." Nothing heavy and theological about that. Very little that is dogmatic, technically, about it. Just that here is a shepherd who loves his sheep, and one of the sheep in doing the most natural thing in the world—and that is to eat the grass—did it with such enthusiasm and over a time interval of such duration that he didn't know when the shepherd called, and he was lost.

And why was he lost? He was lost because he was out of touch, out of touch. That's why he was lost. Out of touch with the group that sustained him, the group that fed him, that gave him a sense that he counted. That's all. And as soon as he was out there alone, he said, "I'm just here by myself. Nothing but me in all of this? And I want to feel that I count with the others." There's a certain warmth in that. There's a certain something that is creative and redemptive about the sense of community, about the fellowship.

Now I call your attention to two things about that. The first is that this lost sheep wasn't a bad sheep. And what he did was not a bad thing. It became a deadly thing, however. When [in eating the grass], or in quest of it, he unwittingly paid the price of being cut off from the rest.

Now, there are many of us that are lost that way. Have you ever heard anyone say, "I can stand on my own two feet"? You have heard that. You have heard people say that, "While it's nice that I have the good feeling of other people and the sense of belonging,...I don't need anybody. I don't *need* anybody. Only the weak need other people. If you are a man or if you a woman, you can stand on your own feet and be autonomous and independent. For if you're dependent upon anybody, then you place your life at the disposal of their whims." A lot of sense in that. But it is true, isn't it my friends, that nobody wants to be insulated; you can't stand being insulated, and that is why, you see, the whole dimension of the meaning of the parable shifts, for the thing to which our attention is called in the dress of the parable is a physical proximity...but, as we think about it, it's insulation. Insulation is something that is spiritual; it is something that inside of me—and I don't know that I can make this as clear as I think I see it—but there's something inside of me that pulls up the moat, the

drawbridge, I mean—[laughs] I didn't mean it that way—
that pulls up the drawbridge so that I'm on my little island.
And sometimes I do it because I'm afraid; sometimes I do
it because I'm clumsy and awkward, and I don't quite know
how to establish a relationship or relationships with my fellows that can float my spirit to them and bring their spirit
to me.

When a nation discovers that it is finally insulated, I
don't care how weak the nation is, how poor the nation is,
when a nation realizes that it is completely insulated, it goes
to war. That is the history of our whole civilization, of our
whole country, isn't it? We can't stand being cut off.

Now, what is salvation? Salvation is reestablishing one's
sense of belonging. You see, every person is specifically related to . . . [missing].

Now, Jesus says that God is like the shepherd, seeking
always to find those who are out of community with their
fellows, and when they have found it, when they have found
their community with their fellows, then all the world
seems to fit back into place, and life takes on a new meaning. Have you ever had the experience of being cut off
from some fellowship, some community, and then all during the time that you are cut off nothing seems to be right?
The sun isn't as bright as it should be. Life isn't quite right.
And then, you are restored. And when you're restored, a
lot of things seem to fall into place. Now that can be not
only in terms of human relations but it can be in terms of
dimensions of community of feeling and thought that restore meaning and value to your very life, as illustrated, for
instance, in the very great speech that appears in Bernard
Shaw's *St. Joan*, when they say to her, "We'll burn you at the
stake," and she takes the document and tears it up, and
then she says, "I won't recant, for if I recant then you're
going to lock me in a dungeon where I can't see the sunlight, where I cannot breathe, where I cannot be a part of

the movement of life that sustains me. It is better to die at the stake than to be cut off from the things that give me a sense of community as a dignified, meaningful human being." And that is why the inner attitude is so important, for if I am unyielding, if I am embittered, if I am unforgiving, if I have bitterness that I cannot relax, then those things stand between me and the things that feed my spirit. And I can't seek release from God until I'm willing to seek release from you.

The lost sheep. The searching shepherd. And the cry of anguish of the sheep was the voice of identification that the shepherd heard. That is how God is, if we let him.

3

THE PRODIGAL SON

(Luke 15:11–32)

Once again, Thurman delves into the heart of a parable, a "simple story" that is "simply told" yet utterly profound, an expression of how Jesus envisioned the nature of God and the nature of fellowship, the nature of community, with God and with others.

Thurman's keen eyes and receptive ears lead him to see and hear in this parable what is abundantly clear, what is artfully implied, and what is missing. Some elements Thurman mentions but does not pursue, like the mother of the prodigal who is notable only by her absence. Or the "consummate touch of genius" of Jesus the storyteller who has the prodigal travel to a "far county" and who ends up as a "keeper of hogs," which for a Jewish man demonstrates just how far out of the community that sustains him he has traveled.

The parable itself is famously open-ended: We are not told, for example, whether the elder son eventually acquiesces to his father's pleas and goes inside to celebrate the return of his brother. In addition, Thurman does not focus on what many interpreters see as the younger son's repentance: the "came to his senses" (15:17) of the parable is just as ambiguous as "it occurred to him" in Thurman's retelling. Thus Thurman recognizes, unlike many interpreters, that we cannot be certain in the parable itself whether the younger son actually repents; although the larger Lukan context implies it, the parable itself does not.

In the context of the parable itself, the younger son may again be manipulating his father. When the younger son asked for his inheritance prematurely, for example, he played his father for a fool. Likewise, the wording in the parable makes it unclear whether his realization (when he "comes to his senses") constitutes repentance or is merely a plan of action to make sure he does not starve; readers of the parable can raise significant questions about his motives and sincerity. Thurman, however, does not explicitly question the prodigal's sincerity; for him, the main problem, the most important thing, was that the son had forgotten that he was his father's son. He had lost his family and his community, but now he was coming home.

God is like the father, anyone can be like the prodigal, and anyone can be like the elder brother. We are meant to be in fellowship with God; we are meant to be in a family relationship with God our Father, but we can become estranged from God, whether or not we ever "leave home." But God, like the father in the parable, always makes the first move: seeking, searching, welcoming, and receiving us back into that family relationship.

Thurman's next point is both insightful and somewhat puzzling, and he wisely cautions us not to "push [it] that far": that there can be a relationship between one's external environment and one's inmost thoughts and feelings: "The clue to the outer is the inner." This reflection about the outer reflecting the inner leads us to a major conviction and core belief of Thurman, one that reflects both insights of Jesus and insights from Hinduism:

> "When [the prodigal] came to himself," he came to his father. That when I...come to the very center, the very core of myself, then I come face to face with God. That God is, God is within me. That he is the very point of my being and existence...[T]hat there is of man which is God. Not a reflection of God. Not some staggering accent of God, but that which is God.

This personal transformation, the coming to oneself and therefore coming to God, is the foundational first step that leads to all other transformations of self and society. One's personal, inner transformation should lead to social action. Such social transformation is possible because of our own inner transformation and the guiding hand of God our father.

The Prodigal Son

September 23, 1951

Meditation and Prayer

My heart an altar; thy love the flame. The patience of unanswered prayer. The dimness of the soul removed. It is good once again to gather in the quietness and to center down in stillness. The streets of our minds are so filled with traffic. Our spirits are so crowded with conflicting noises that it is wonderful to be quiet and to see if in the quietness we cannot sense some order in our lives, some specific sense of direction, something that will tend to structure our confusion so that we may understand its character. In the quietness we may look at ourselves, the kinds of people we are. What are the kinds of things that we are doing, and why are we doing them? What is the whole point of our functioning? Where are we trying to go? What is it that we are meaning by what we do, and what is the point of our kind of living? Where do we put the emphasis in our lives? Or each may make it very personal: Where do I put the emphasis in my life? What am I after? Where are my values placed? To what end am I making my peculiar kind of sacrifice? What is it that I love most in life? What is it that I despise most in life? To what am I true, and why am I true to it? Who am I anyway? Who am I, and what am I doing? And as we listen, is all we get the jangling echo of our own confusion and chaos? Or is there something more, some deeper note that we have not heard before because we have not been still enough to listen? To listen, until all the sounds are defined. To listen, until we are quiet enough to hear the whisper in the heart. And what does it say to us? What does it say?

Spirit of God, descend upon our hearts, wean [them] from earth, through all [their] pulses move. Amen.

SERMON

Before I begin our sermon this morning, I'd like to make a statement, and it really doesn't apply to those who are involved this morning because I'm sure ... [missing] recall your attention last Sunday, and eventually what appears as a sermon topic and what the preacher talks about will get together. This last Sunday you will recall, we thought together about the teaching, the parable, the parables which have to do with the lost coin and the lost sheep, parables which indicated somewhat the mind of Jesus in an effort to answer to his own satisfaction and to the satisfaction of his hearers the question of what is God like and also an effort on his part to deal with the meaning of the relationship of the human spirit to God, which is, after all, the fundamental point of all religion.

For the religious endeavor of the human spirit is to underwrite the significance of salvation, however it may be defined. That is its point. And the story with which we have to do this morning is a familiar one. Simply told, it is the story of a boy who was younger, and a boy who was older, and a father. A family, but a family in which the mother does not appear. It's very interesting. The boy who [was] young said to his father, "Give me what is coming to me now so that I can go away. I want to try my wings." And his father gave him what was coming to him, and he went away.

And Jesus puts in a very interesting touch. [The boy] went into a far country, and there he met many friends, friends who liked his personality, liked his way with money, and they enjoyed him thoroughly as to his surplus. And then he [ran] out of money. And that is perfectly natural in time, and he looked for his friends, friends who had enjoyed his money, and he thought they were enjoying him, and he looked for them, and he found them not.

But he had to eat. And it's interesting that when his hunger became sufficiently great, he was willing to pay almost any price as to his pride, as to his self-respect, in order that he might get food. So, he went to hire himself out to a man as a keeper of his hogs, which is a consummate touch of genius on the part of Jesus, that this [boy] who was a Jewish [person] as to his faith, as Jesus was, and he was so far beyond the reach of the climate that sustained him that he in his desperation became a herder of hogs and a feeder of hogs, and not only that, but he ate some of the food that he was feeding the hogs.

And while he was in that state, it occurred to him that he was his father's son. He'd forgotten that. And so he said, "I will go to my father, and I will not let my pride stand in the way. I will just tell him what I have been doing, the kind of person I am, and tell him I don't want to be his son any more, but I want to be as one of the hired servants, because it is better to be a hired servant of my father than to be in the far country stranded and alone, all surrounded by sunshine friends."

But his father saw him coming and ran out to meet him, so that the boy didn't have a chance to say, "Father so on, so on, so make me as one of the hired servants." The only thing that the boy had a chance to say was, "I'm so sorry, and I realize now that I didn't do this against anyone but against you and against myself, really." His father fell on his neck and kissed him. He was so glad to see him that in that swirling moment of heightened ecstasy, he said to his servants, "Get the special garment, kill the fatted calf, wash him, and bring him in here so that he can know that he is at the center of my heart where he's been all the time."

And then the older boy came home, and he heard all of this. And he said, "I wonder what's going on?" And he listened, and he said, "Oh yes; he's back. I knew he was coming back." He didn't say, "Gee, how wonderful it is that he's back, and now a smile will be on my father's face again." No, [he said], "All the time he was away having a good time, I was right here working. It seems as if the way to win your spurs with my father is to go off and throw things away, and then you get the central place. But if you stay and work, then you get no credit for it."

And his rumbling was so significant that he spoke to his father, and he said, "I've been here all the time, and you have never had a party for me. You never said, 'Kill the fatted calf.'" And the father said, "Everything that I have is yours, my boy, but can't you understand? Can't you feel your way into some sensitiveness as to what is taking place in me and in your brother? He was lost, and now he's found. Can you understand what that is? Now I can die in peace, because I have seen my child again."

Now that's the story. A simple story. And I don't want to take the time and make it all complex and complicated, but I have three things I want to say about it.

The first is merely to state what it seems to me the teaching says in the context and in the spirit of Jesus. The teaching says that God is like that father, and that anybody may be like the prodigal son, and anybody may be like the older brother. We all stand in that relationship, the family relationship with God, and you are lost if you are out of primary fellowship with God, whatever else you may have. And you may be out of primary fellowship with God without ever going away from home. For the older boy didn't ever go away from home, [but] he was out of fellowship nevertheless. Be careful, then, how you live, for you are lost if you are out of fellowship with God. Now that's what he is saying, and anytime you start moving in that direction, the first thing that you discover is that all the time God has been moving toward you. Now that's the story. That's all there is to it. But it's a great deal. Now we will move to part two.

Now the first thing in part two is this: One of the things that stirred in my mind, that always stirs in my mind as I read it, because it is profoundly puzzling to me, and it is a part of experience, but I don't quite know altogether what it means. But the fact that in the story that Jesus tells ... there seems to be a relationship between what is going on in the external environment or in the environment in which we are living and what is going on inside of us. Now, this is the thing that is suggested to my mind: that the famine that the boy experienced in the far country was a part also of the famine that he was experiencing inside himself. I am constantly puzzled and disturbed by the way in which we seem to surround ourselves with the kind of environment or aura or climate that seems to be a reflection of the kind of thing that is going on inside of us. Now without seeming to be superstitious, I cannot put down the reflection that it is not an accident that we pick up the newspapers day after day, and perfectly good, well-disciplined, and well-organized airplanes just drop, crash, just a rash of them for the last two or three years. What does that mean? I don't know what it means. But let's play with this a little with our minds and spirits, because there's something here. I was reading a report the other day by some doctor of the mind in which he pointed out the interesting relationship between the number of people who suffer from automobile accidents, from all sorts of accidents having to do with coordination and so forth and so on, the striking corollary between them and their inner mental and spiri-

tual confusion, and he does a disturbing thing: he lists from
his files of his—whatever it's called, his records—the number of patients who had come to him, and who had been
treated by him, and the number of those patients who in
their history had brought with them accountings of accidents, of things that point up a kind of outer balance with
the environment.

Now don't, don't push that too far. Don't let your
minds go back now to an accident that a friend of yours
had the other day and so you knew that something was
wrong with that person all along [laughter], and now is the
moment when it gets vindicated, but, no, it makes a certain
kind of sense that there is, that, that, that—how to say
this!—that the climate that surrounds us is not unrelated to
the kind of climate that is inside of us. Now we see it in simple ways. Have you ever gotten up in the morning feeling
depressed because you did not sleep well or because of any
one of a half dozen things, and you go about your regular
daily tasks, whatever they may be, and you discover that
there's some kind of contagion between this thing inside of
you, this down feeling inside of you, and the way various individuals in your environment respond to you, the way the
world looks to you? Or have you not at sometimes had a
great updraft of wonderful inner resurgence of creative
spirit and feeling, and then suddenly it burst upon you that
this is a beautiful world? Hasn't it happened to you?
There's something there. Therefore, it seems to be relevant
to say that the most important clue to my outside world is
my inside world.

On one of the facades of the railway station in Washington, DC, there is the statement, "He who seeks the wealth
of the Indies must carry the wealth of the Indies with him."
That's the insight that's at work there. That's what Jesus is
talking about. Or that wonderful medieval mystic of Hinduism who says that "I laugh when you say that a fish in the
water is thirsty. Do you seek the real? Go where you will,

from Benares to Mathara. If you have not found your own soul, the world is unreal to you." Now that isn't the whole story, but that is so crucially a part of the whole story that it is worth calling your attention to. That the clue to the outer is the inner. The famine that the boy experienced in the far country he was already experiencing in his own heart. It's very simple.

Now, the other thing I wanted to say is: he came to himself. And this follows that: he came to himself. And when he came to himself, he came to his father. When he came to himself, he came to his father. That when I, what that says is, when I come to the very center, the very core of myself, then I come face to face with God. That God is, God is within me. That he is the very point of my being and my existence. Now I know that that sounds commonplace, and [it] sounds as if it is the same thing that is being said over and over again. And perhaps it is. But when Jesus insists that the door to the father of the prodigal son could not open until the boy opened it down inside of him, that there is that of man which is God. Not a reflection of God. Not some staggering accent of God, but that which is God. So when I raise the question as to what am I, I know that I'm this or that or the other, but when I am most myself, I know that there is something in me that for lack of a better term I will call that which is otherworldly, otherworldly. Think about yourself for a moment. You know that you have appetites; you have a body; you have a mind ... [missing] that it is so important to be as adequately expressive of myself as possible. I think that is why it is so important for young people, for instance, who are growing into life to get a tool, to take the time, to find a tool, to fashion a tool that will be vehicular for them, that will be the means by which they can provide an escalator from the churning spirit that is within them to the external world. Even though when they do the best they can it is inadequate, it

is limited, and because in the very nature of the case it is
limited, it places a heavier responsibility upon making the
tool the most exacting thing that the spirit can devise or
the mind can create, so that when I have done my best, I
know it will be less than what I wanted to express, but it will
be a full and adequate manifestation of the equipment that
I have. That's why it is so important when you are young to
do the thing, to do the learning, the disciplining, to review
the possibilities and select some expression of your life that
will structure it for even after you have lived to the full,
doing to the limit of your power all that your wisdom and
experience and judgment and technique and competency
can inspire, at the end of your days, even though you may
be covered with the glory of men, deep in your heart you
will know that you didn't do it, and, therefore, therefore,
if coupled with the feeling that when I have done my best
I have failed to reveal that which is stirring most deeply
within me, how terrible it is if, in addition to that, I feel
that I have wasted my time and my energy, failed to select
a tool that will express this thing that cannot be expressed,
but I cannot ever be excused from the awful responsibility
of trying to express it.

And it is never too late to find the tool. I can always say,
well, I'm too old to find the tool; I am too limited; I am too
this, too that. That is no excuse. I think I have told you—
and I will be through in a minute—I think I have told you
about one of the most moving stories that Rufus Jones told
me when I worked with him, about a South China, Maine,
farmer, a very illiterate farmer, who had a concern, and that
concern was to establish a Quaker hostel somewhere in
Palestine. And when he went to First Day Meeting and told
the people about it, they listened in the quietness, and each
one had his private smile, and there was no assent from
them, no consent of the meeting, or whatever the technical
phrase is. Then he went to the Quarterly Meeting and told

the same thing, and there he met the same quiet rejection, because the whisper in their hearts had included the fact that this man [was] sincere, but he [was] illiterate. So he went to the Annual Meeting, and the same thing happened. Then he went to the Five Year Meeting, and the same thing happened, and then at that time, he sold his farm and went to Palestine and established the hostel.

That's what I'm talking about. For the moment, deep within you, you come to yourself, you find waiting there your father, who can take your limitations, all of the broken manifestations of your day's or year's journey and brood over them with his infinite wisdom, tenderness, and knowledge of the whole meaning of existence and place at your disposal that which will make you his son. That is yours. That's mine. And I'm grateful to God that it is so. Grateful, grateful to God that I'm his son, and he's my father.

4

FORGIVENESS

The Two Debtors (Luke 7:36-50)
and the Unmerciful Servant (Matthew 18:23-35)

*The two parables that Thurman explores in this sermon
offer similar portraits of the grace and forgiveness of God,
including the human responsibilities that result from receiving God's grace/forgiveness. George Buttrick's* Parables of
Jesus, *one of the resources Thurman used to provide historical and other contexts for this sermon, also categorizes
these two parables in the same section: "Marks of Discipleship: Forgiven and Forgiving," which appropriately corre-
sponds to Thurman's thoughts on being forgiven and
forgiving others.[1]*

*It is possible if not probable that the woman "who was
a sinner" was a prostitute. Other options are also possible,
although her kissing and anointing Jesus's feet most likely
would have been understood by the people at the dinner
as sexually inappropriate if not shockingly so. And, as
Thurman notes, the later church tradition that identifies*

---

1. George A. Buttrick, *The Parables of Jesus* (New York: Richard
R. Smith, 1930), 92–102. Buttrick's book is also reflected in Thurman's
comments in other places in the sermon, such as how people could
walk in the house uninvited and listen to the discussion at dinner (94),
and how ten thousand talents were worth approximately two million
dollars (100).

her as "Mary" (usually Mary Magdalene) is most certainly incorrect.[2]

The Greek word used for the forgiveness of debts in the parable is charizomai, *which has as its foundation the word for "grace"* (charis), *a word that often implies graciousness, kindness, and goodwill on the part of the giver and also a sense of favor, thankfulness, and gratitude on the part of the receiver.*[3] *In the case of the two-debtors parable, the one who receives more* charis *in return feels more gratitude.*[4] *Or, as Thurman puts it, "The measure of my sense of need for forgiveness is the measure of my outgoing need to meet the forgiveness in others." The more we realize our own shortcomings and failings, the more forgiving we should be of the shortcomings and failings of others. As Thurman notes, the story and its moral are "very simple," although, one might add, it is also easier said than done.*

---

2. Here Thurman correctly disagrees with Buttrick's *Parables of Jesus,* which identifies the woman as "Mary" (94). Thurman's informed perspective on the Pharisees also demonstrates his familiarity with historical scholarship about them; he recognizes, for example, that the "judgmental attitude" toward Pharisees in the New Testament does not really reflect "the genius of the Pharisaic movement in Israel." One of the key works on which Thurman relied was Louis Finkelstein's classic work, *The Pharisees* (Philadelphia: The Jewish Publication Society of America, 1938).

3. Henry Liddell and Robert Scott, "charis," in *Greek-English Lexicon,* seventh edition (Oxford: Oxford University Press, 1978), 882.

4. First-century readers/hearers would also place this forgiveness of debt into the category of *patronage,* a foundational element of first-century Mediterranean societies. A "patron" is someone who provides a benefit or blessing to a "client," someone on a lower socio-economic level. In return, the client is expected to reciprocate in some fashion (e.g., through expressions of gratitude or deference to the patron). God, of course, is the ultimate patron. See, for example, S. N. Eisenstadt and Louis Roniger, eds., *Patrons, Clients, and Friends* (Cambridge: Cambridge University Press, 1984).

Thurman acknowledges the all-too-human tendency to want mercy for ourselves and to desire "justice" for (judgment upon) others in similar situations. Since God showers human beings with grace and forgiveness, however, human beings should follow God's lead in their relationships with each other, showing the same type of grace, compassion, and forgiveness to each other, in debts large and small. In fact, as Thurman observes, we can expect forgiveness for our own transgressions only when we are willing to forgive others for their transgressions against us.

FORGIVENESS

September 30, 1951

MEDITATION

There are some who seek sustenance and support for grand plans and great undertakings that have excited their minds and stimulated their adventure. Some who seek the power and the strength to forgive someone who has wronged them.

> Our Father who art in heaven
> Hallowed by thy name
> Thy kingdom come
> Thy will be done on earth as it is in heaven.
> Give us this day our daily bread
> And forgive our debts as we forgive our debtors.
> And lead us not into temptation but deliver us from
> evil.
> For thine is the kingdom and the power and the
> glory forever. Amen

The continuation of our thinking together about the parables. This morning we are dealing with two of the very striking parables of Jesus. And they have to do with forgiveness of sin. Very simple stories, they are. One of them has a dramatic setting. A Pharisee—and I hope that you will bear in mind that most of the New Testament references to the Pharisees are references that reflect a judgmental attitude toward the Pharisee that [does not acknowledge] . . . the genius of the Pharisaic movement in Israel. It is a reflection of another kind of attitude, [a] kind of prejudice, and this of course is nothing new, nothing radical; it's an old familiar thing to those persons who have made any study of either the Pharisees or the Sadducees or of Israel or of the life of Jesus for that matter.

But there stands a Pharisee, nevertheless. And he invited Jesus along with his other friends to dinner. And in those days, you ate with an exposure to the street, that is, the room had an exposure to the street. Strangers could drop in if they walked by, and they saw you in there eating, and they remembered they wanted to talk with you about something, that was a good time to talk with you. You are relaxed, and you are in a good mood, and if the food is good, you are apt to [have] a positive and favorable reaction. So people came in and out as the case may have been.

And then, while everybody was eating and everything was lovely, this woman came in. And it was very interesting because time stood still when she appeared. And why did time stand still? Because every man there, every person there, every guest, including Jesus himself, knew what kind of woman she was. And in ordinary language, she was a woman of the street. A prostitute. Now here is the setting: here is a Pharisee, the host, on the one hand, Jesus the guest, and the woman. And what do you think was going on in everybody's mind? It's an interesting question. And evidently great was the relief when the woman came in and she went straight to Jesus. And that was when Simon drew a sigh of relief. But it faced him with another problem: when the woman came to Jesus, she fell at his feet, pulled the pin out of her hair, and it fell over on his feet, covering his feet. And, according to this picture, she kissed his feet, the ultimate act of humility and self-abasement, the radical and dramatic expression of a sense of unworthiness. And under the cover of her hair, her eyes became fountains of tears as she bathed his feet with the tears of her anguish.

And then everybody began reacting, and they said, "You have no right to be here. This is no place for you. You are outside of the pale, outside of the protection and the guarantors of respectability." Some man writing about her said—and he calls her by the name Mary, but I think that's a mistake, but nevertheless, this is what he said—

> Once I was white as the snow,
> but I fell like a snowflake from heaven to hell,
> fell to be trampled as filth in the street,
> fell to be laughed at, spit on, and beat,
> cursing, pleading, dreading to die,
> selling my soul to whoever would buy.
> Dealing in shame, for a morsel of bread,
> hating the living and fearing the dead.
> All merciful God, have I fallen so low,
> and once I was pure as the beautiful snow?[5]

Then Jesus took over, and what did he do? He told a story...a story. He said there was a man who... Let me read the story to you:

---

5. The poem is "Beautiful Snow," which is attributed to John Whitaker Watson, 1871.

And Jesus answering said unto him, "Simon, I have something to say unto thee." And he said, "Master, say on." "There was a certain creditor who had two debtors. The one owed five hundred pence, and the other fifty. And when they had nothing to pay, he frankly forgave them both. Tell me, therefore, which of them will love him most." And Simon said, "Well I suppose that he to whom he forgave most." And he said unto him, "Thou hast rightly judged." And he turned to the woman, and he said unto him, "Simon, seest thou this woman? I entered into thine house, thou gavest me no water for my feet. She hath washed my feet with tears, and wiped them with the hairs of her head. Thou gavest me no kiss, but this woman since the time I came in has not ceased to kiss my feet. My head with oil thou didst not anoint, and this woman hath anointed my feet with ointment. Wherefore I say unto thee, her sins which are many are forgiven, for she loved much, but to whom little is forgiven, the same loveth little.

—Luke 7:40–47 (KJV)

And that's the story. The measure of my sense of need for forgiveness is the measure of my outgoing to meet the need for forgiveness in others. Very simple. Very simple.

Now there is one little question I would like to raise before I go to the second [parable]. One little question. Why is it that the person who gives you the most trouble seems to get closest to your heart? Do you believe that? Were you one of two or three children in the family, and you were very good? So you don't know what I am talking about [laughter], but the child that was always in difficulties, and I thought about it a great deal. Of course if you are a parent you spend more time talking, parents spend more time talking together about the child that's giving them trouble.

Isn't that right? They do more soul-searching about that. Because one of the things they are trying to do, it seems to me, is to be sure that they can rid themselves of a feeling of guilt about it. Because even though they know that the child got these discrepancies out of the blue, that they didn't come from any kind of inheritance or any lack of parental guidance and example [laughter]. But where did they come from? They must have come from somewhere, and then you look at each other [laughter], and you know that, well, and then you talk about other aspects of it. But the result is that more of you has to be given as the whole part of you tracks down the limitations and the inadequacies of the loved one and wraps its health around it, hoping that redemption will be possible. And you never give up.

Now if it happens that the person feels consciously in need of forgiveness, then the new dimension of the possibilities of redemption takes place. For you see, even where you are dealing with an individual who is stubborn and unyielding and recalcitrant, who has no sense of the need for forgiveness, yet if you love, the love envelops and keeps trying to break down the inner resistance of the other person until that person from within starts moving from there toward you to meet the great creative love which you hold in your heart. But if there is a stirring in the other person, if the other person has a need, a sense [of a] need for forgiveness and tries to work it out, tries to move toward the health that is being offered to him, then love becomes magnificent.

Now the person who should be most sensitive to the needs of others, most sensitive to the transgressions of others, is the person who is most deeply conscious of his own transgressions. There is no more tragic person in the world than a person who is incapable of having a sense of error in him. Have you ever seen anybody like that? You may be mistaken, but that person is never mistaken. You know how difficult it is to get to them? Have you ever tried? Thank God

I'm pure [laughter]. Have you ever had to deal with someone like that? Not a chance.

Now the second parable grows right out of this one.
That parable is of a man who owed a vast sum of money. If
you measured the scriptural reference in terms of dollars,
it would be something like two million dollars. And he said
to the man to whom he owed the money, "I'm very sorry,
but I can't pay it, it's more than I can pay, more than I can
ever pay." And the man to whom he was indebted said,
"Well, all right. If you can't do it, then let's forget it. Let's
forget it. I'll wipe it off and let you start all over again with
your life. I will not handicap you further with a burden that
you can't carry." "Oh thank you so much. Now I can go on
living." And when he walked around the corner, he ran into
a man who owed him about two dollars and a quarter
[laughter]. And he said, "I've been looking all over for you"
[laughter]. And this man said, "Well you know, I was trying
to find you. I'm very sorry, but I can't pay you. I don't have
it." Well, you know what he said: "I must have mine!"

Oh, Jesus was wonderful, wasn't he? He just knew, he
could just put his finger right on the spotlight so it could
turn its rays on when you weren't expecting any light at all.
If it is something that I owe you, I want mercy; if you owe
me, I want mine!

How perfectly natural that is. And why is it true? Because it is so difficult for us to deal honestly with ourselves.
When I watch you do something, I'm apt to have an attitude of judgment toward it and toward you and toward the
doing of it; but when I do that thing, then I deal with it in
an entirely different manner. If I try to get everything I can
for myself, I'm just being wise, protecting myself against a
rainy day. If you try to do it, then you're unscrupulous,
you're an exploiter, you're X, you're Y. It's curious, isn't it?

Now Jesus says something very simple: that I can only
seek forgiveness from God for the sins which I have committed, for the error, if I am willing to forgive people for

the things they do to me. You believe that? You believe that? That if I am hard-hearted, if I'm unyielding, if I insist that the thing that happened to me was so terrible that I can't forgive you, then every time I fall upon my unrepentant knees, either actually or figuratively, seeking the forgiveness of God in order that my own spirit may have a sense of freedom, of movement, then the thing that stands between me and that forgiveness is your face. I can't get to God, because every time I start, you are in the way. There is only one way I can get you out of my path, and that is "to forgive you out." And until I do that I can't get to God.

Jesus illustrated it in another way: That in going to the temple to bring your gift, if when you get to the temple with your gift, you remember that your brother has aught against you, not that you have aught against your brother— it's easy for you remember that, because you can't forget that—but you remember that your brother has aught against you. That somebody is holding this thing against you, and you know it, and you say, "Well, it isn't my fault. Just let him do it, I'm not responsible for that." But Jesus says that if you remember that someone has aught against you, leave your gift—don't try to fool God; don't do that. That doesn't help things. Leave your gift; go and find the person, find the person who has this ill-will against you, and then work out a reconciliation.

And that is very instructive, because there is no experience in which you have been injured by another person in which you do not share some of the guilt. There is no such thing as a one-sided judgment in that particular. Examine carefully under the light of your best judgment and your most enlightened wisdom the situation of conflict that you are having right now with someone; think about it for a moment, if you are having one and you're sure that all the guilt is on one side. If you examine it very carefully, you will discover that you share the responsibility, that much, so much that is not good, has flown from you to other people,

[and] that more and more as you deepen your own sense of religious values and spiritual experience, more and more you will learn that you must be gracious toward other people, for so much that is not good flows from them to you.

You are not without guilt, and, therefore, no forgiveness can take place unless it is mutual. The person who has injured me, yes, I can only forgive him when in my own heart and mind with great honesty I ask him to forgive me. And then when I do that, I can pray to God asking God to forgive me even as I forgive others. And if you are the kind of person who doesn't pray, [and] then therefore what I am saying about praying to God for forgiveness is the thing you don't do, and therefore [think] this does not involve you, you're just mistaken. Because sooner or later you will come to your knees seeking something that will so operate on your insides that you will be free again. That you might have less heaviness of heart, that you may be able to look into the eyes of another person or that person and feel no ill-will, no judgment, that whatever the process is by which that takes place in you, it adds up to this: that you are trying in the process so to settle your account with life that life will begin to flow freely through you again.

And in the language of religion, that is the forgiveness of God. And if I don't seek it, I can't get along, because no one of us is free from hurting other people, and every time you do, you throw out of line the relationship that guarantees your sense of wholeness. And you can't be yourself as long as you hold in yourself the kind of thoughts and attitudes that keep other people from being themselves.

I seek the forgiveness of God not because I'm worthy of it, but because it is the only practical way by which I can live without an increasing disintegration.

5

THE GOOD SAMARITAN

(Luke 10:25-37)

Thurman's reflections on Jesus's "very simple story" of the Good Samaritan in Luke's Gospel are, like the parable itself, simply profound. The parable, Thurman declares, breaks down the barriers that divide us, the lines that every culture draws between those who belong and those who do not, the lines human beings draw to develop their individuality and identity in the world, the lines human beings draw to separate and protect themselves from "the impersonal operations of nature" and "the impersonal operations of society."[1]

Jesus proclaims an understanding of "neighbor," Thurman argues, that insists that we all—every single one of us—are related to one another. Being a neighbor goes beyond sharing things in common, whether kinship, race, or creed. For Jesus, being a neighbor doesn't even mean responding to a person's need, which, in effect, can be responding to our own need of feeling good about ourselves or expecting to be recognized or rewarded for our good deed.

Thurman therefore insists that Jesus's concept of being a neighbor means that we actively relate ourselves to one another. We are to love one another in the sense of being

---

1. Thurman extends significantly Buttrick's insights about relating to each other as "humans." George A. Buttrick, *The Parables of Jesus* (New York: Richard R. Smith, 1930), 152–54.

"involved in an encounter that leads from the core of me to the core of you," despite our limitations, despite whatever is good or bad about us, despite any and every thing, we encounter each other as we are. That is the way we are to relate to one another because that is the way God relates to us—in community and fellowship with one another. It definitely is not easy, but when we diligently work and strive to relate ourselves to one another in the way Jesus demands, a new world of possibilities opens up. Just imagine, Thurman ponders, how different our world would be if we all diligently tried to follow the far too lonely path trodden by the Good Samaritan.

THE GOOD SAMARITAN

October 7, 1951

MEDITATION AND PRAYER

How hard it is to make a pause to come to a moment or a season of quiet because our lives are so crowded with things to do with a wide variety of considerations and problems and issues. The stark necessities that come from the struggle for bread, for shelter, for clothing, the vast energies consumed in trying to get along in life and with life, the ways in which the privacy of our inward parts are invaded by suffering, by illness, by the general climate of despair that surrounds our world. It is often very hard to come to a quiet place in one's own mind. There is fighting for control of our minds and hearts, all of the involvements of our daily activities and our daily struggles. We welcome this moment of quiet when the external surrounding seems to suggest that this is a moment for centering down, for settling in, for gathering into one point of focus what it is that we are after, what are the deep desires of our hearts, what do we think is the meaning of life, the meaning of our own lives, how are we related to ourselves, to the things that we do everyday, to those with whom we live, how are we related to our God. It is wonderful to pause, to be quiet, to feel one's way gingerly into the secret place of one's own heart. To be quiet. To make an end of activity. To rest, perchance to be refreshed and renewed.

O God, our Father, who looks with such infinite under-standing and longsuffering upon the foibles of our lives. Be very near us in the quietness of this place, that for one swirling moment we may see ourselves as thou dost see us, stripped to the literal substance of ourselves without pre-tense, without all of the boasting, without all of the façades by which we maneuver our days. O God, our Father, teach us how we may understand the movement of thy spirit in our hearts as it leads us in the traffic of life to move with the strength and the independence of solitude. This is the way we feel as we wait in thy presence, O God, our Father. Amen.

SERMON

This morning we pick up the threads of our series of think-ing together on the parables of Jesus, and today we are dealing with the parable that is perhaps most familiar to all persons acquainted with the Bible: the story of the Good Samaritan. It's a very simple story, simply and directly told by Jesus. There was a man who raised a very searching ques-tion. He was a lawyer, as touching his faith, and the rest of it. He said to Jesus, "What may I do to inherit eternal life?" It's very interesting how he cannot easily escape the neces-sity for insisting that you pay for everything you get, on the one hand, and the persistent temptation to try to get every-thing without paying for it. It's a curious thing, isn't it? On the one hand, we assume that you pay for everything you get, and since that's true, one of the games of life, it seems, is to try to prove that it isn't true.

"What shall I do to inherit eternal life?" And Jesus told him, "You know what the law says, what does the law say about it?" And he quoted the great, timeless utterance about loving God with all one's mind, heart, soul, and strength, and loving one's neighbor as oneself. And when Jesus insisted that he should go and do that, then the man raised another question: "Granted that it is true that I should love my neighbor as myself, how am I to determine who is my neighbor?"

And in reply to that question, Jesus told a simple story. That a certain man went along a certain road. It was a very dangerous road, from Jerusalem down to Jericho. And he fell among thieves, and thieves did to him what thieves would do. They took what he had, and he didn't like it so much. He resisted, apparently, so they injured him, and left him stripped of his goods, and also sick, wounded. And along the way came a priest who did not take any cognizance of his presence or condition. The great phrase is that he walked by on the other side; much has been done with that. It's a nice phrase. And then another man came along, [a man] who was, in a sense, a kind of assistant to the priest, who represented also a whole hierarchy of cultural influences of his own, and he walked by without paying any attention to the destitute man by the roadside. And then a third man came by who was a Samaritan. A Samaritan was a man who, in the minds of many of the people who were listening to the story that Jesus told, . . . lived on the other side of the tracks. He was almost there but wasn't quite there. So this Samaritan ministered to the needs of this helpless man by pouring oil and wine on his wounds, cleaning him up, and then he put him on his donkey and carried him to a little resting place, an inn, that evidently was protected, and he said to the innkeeper, "Now take care of this man, and any expenses beyond the money that I am giving you now that are involved, I will repay you when I return." And Jesus said that the man who befriended the destitute individual was the man who showed the neighborly attitude.

That's a very simple story. Very simple. Who is my neighbor, according to the story? Any man whose need calls me, and I respond to that need.

Now that's all. Now let's work at it for a little. There are two or three observations that I would make about this simple story. And the first observation is the recognition of the fact that it is a part of the pattern of cultures and civilizations to make a radical distinction between those who belong and those who not belong. One of the reasons why I think that the goals of religion, certainly this kind of religion about which Jesus is insisting, the goals of religion and the goals of civilization must of necessity be mutually exclusive goals. For states, for civilizations, for cultures [to] build themselves into positions of security and power and domination [means] seeing to it that a line is drawn between those who are and those who are not. It is an old distinction. Everybody who wasn't a Greek was a barbarian. So even now on college and university campuses, if you are not fortunate enough to be a member of a sorority or a fraternity, you are called a barbarian. You see, if you belong, you are Greek. If you don't belong, you are a barbarian. If you are not a Jew, you are a Gentile. And very recently, if you are not a capitalist, you're a communist [laughter]. It's very interesting. You are either an occidental or you're an oriental. It's an interesting thing. You belong to my group, my class, or you're an outsider. And the corollary that follows from that is that we are involved always, then, in operating on two levels at the same time. One could apparently obtain from those who belong, and then another one obtains from those who do not belong. Now... [there are] things that are happening in the modern world that are cutting away at that, undermining it, but that belongs to another discussion. The separate, those who are and those who are not. Now, there is something to be said for this insistence in cultures and civilizations, so let us not just brush it aside as being irrelevant, completely irrelevant, and insignificant. For one of the ways, you see, by which men are able to build a core of meaning for themselves is to fend away all others whose relation to whom would tend to destroy this sense of self that I am building. It's a curious dilemma, and a very difficult problem. The person develops his individuality by separating himself from the not-self, and by building a kind of world, a little world around himself. It is one of the ways by which we defend ourselves against the impersonal operations of the world of nature by getting a house, and by leveling an area, clearing the land, and pushing back the insistent growth of nature, and protecting ourselves from rain and storm and hail. We make private our lives in order that we might not be destroyed by the impersonal operations of the world of nature. We also make private our lives in relation to society in order that we may not be destroyed by the impersonal operations of society. We relate ourselves to family: "This is my family, not your family. And because this is my family then to that extent those who are not my family represent a level of relatedness to me that is not comparable to the relatedness of my family."

So who is my neighbor? Well, it seems as if the neighbor breaks down into two kinds at once: those that are my neighbor who are of the household of my life and meaning and values, and then if I have anything left, then I share it with those who are next in line. Now that seems to be the pattern.

Now over against that, Jesus comes with another kind of insistence. It is very interesting. His insistence is that I am related to the other person, not to the world of his relations. Now, I wish I had a blackboard, because I am drawing it here [laughter]. We are not related to his position. We are not related to his race. We are not related to his creed. We are not related . . . really, we are not related to his need. But before you disagree, think about it a little. We are not related to his need. We are related to him. To him!

Now the second suggestion that follows from that is that most of our relatedness is in terms of what people symbolize to us, what they are, what they need. Think back now. We need not hurry over this part of it. Think back. When was the last time you gave something to help somebody? You remember? How did you feel? What made you do it? Were you related to that person? Did you relate yourself to that person's need? Or were you trying to say, "I have so much, and I just can't afford not to do this, because God has blessed me, and now I must show my blessing, my gratitude to God for his blessings, by sharing with this person who is in need." Was that the thing? Or did you share because you wanted to have a good night's sleep? And you knew that if you [had] looked on that much human misery and had closed up the bowels of your compassion, something would go out of your life that you needed. So in helping the other person, you were really administering to your own need. Is that it? Is that it? Is that it? Or did you help because if you helped it would put you in line for certain considerations, which you knew down the road you would need? And when the time came, you would reap your rewards. Or did you help because you felt that you were so secure and superior that you could afford to be gracious without undermining either your superiority or your security? What went through your mind when you gave some money to help somebody in need? What would go through your mind when you contribute to the community chest? What would go through your mind? Why would you do it? Why, if you do? Why? Is it because you relate yourself—just this idea—is it because you relate yourself to the other person's need? Or is it because you relate yourself to the other person? There's a difference. There's a difference.

I'll just raise another question, a third, and then we push it on and then tie it up. It seems as if Jesus is insisting that if we relate ourselves to human need, we must draw the line somewhere. If I relate myself to your need, then—or to the needs of those around me—then at some point I must call a halt. Now where do you draw the line? Do you recognize need as long as there [are] available to you resources for meeting that need, which resources are part of your surplus? Or is the line drawn at the point of the other person's need? So that as long as the need persists, whatever I have is at the disposal of the need—not of the person—but of the need? But, of course, human need is infinite, and I can't make a quantitative impression on infinity. The number five bears the same relationship to infinity that the number fourteen million bears. And if human need is infinite, and if I devoted all of my life for a hundred thousand years and all of my resources to the meeting of human need, at the end of that time, the human need remaining would be infinite. So what do I do?

Jesus seems to be insisting that we relate ourselves to the person. I want to talk about that just a little, and I'll be through. And that is the most difficult thing to do. It is when you are related directly to the person that all of the personal, private, ethical problems that are involved in living become crucial. It is so much easier, for instance, to have an attitude of tolerance—if I may use that word—to have an attitude of outgoing understanding toward someone to whom you are not related personally. But when you are related to a person personally, then you are so close up that everything is apt to be magnified. So that it's much [easier] to forgive a national enemy—to shift the scene for a moment—than it is to forgive a personal enemy, because if a person has gotten close enough to you so that you are related to that person, ... there [are] going into the matrix of your relatedness all of the rich overtones of your private living and desiring and fellowship. If all that has happened, then it means that in order to forgive that person, so much more ground has to be covered, because you must forgive at every point of your relatedness.

It's very interesting. That's why when you fall out with your sister, you have such a hard time trying to get that thing straight; or do you? Or when you fall out with your closest friend, have you ever seen the kind of distilled and...

[missing section]

...attitude toward others is that we love them, that we love them, and what does he mean when he says that? He means that when I love, I go beyond the good and the evil in the object of my affection. I deal with the person, not with the fact that he is lovable or unlovable—if there's such a word—not with the fact that he's gifted or not gifted, not with the fact that he's healthy or unhealthy, not with the fact that he's worthy or unworthy, that he's kind or unkind. All of that becomes secondary. The primary thing is that when I say, "I love," it means that I'm involved in an encounter that leads from the core of me to the core of you, past all the good things I know about you, all the attractive things I know about you, beyond all of the bad things I know about you. And it makes contact with the core of you, and standing there, it works back this way to deal with the goodness and the badness. That's why I can never forgive a person if I don't love them that way, because every time I try to deal with the person, I can't get to the person, because I'm blocked by the thing in the person that I can't forgive. So I work up to it, and there it is. I come back, and I go around that way [laughter], and as I move into it, there it is again. And I didn't know it was all over the place. I thought it was right here [laughter]. But not until I can get beyond the good and the evil, beyond the limitations, beyond all of the wonderful things about you and all the bad things about you, until at last, I have a primary and intimate encounter with you, with the very core of you.

And once I do that, then it doesn't matter so much about all these other things. I can look at your goodness, your gifts, your talents, and rejoice without envy or judgment. I can look at your limitations and understand them without condemnation and bitterness. And Jesus says that's the way God deals with human life. And that's the way we are supposed to deal with human life.

What about it? Now, I don't know whether..., I don't know whether it makes sense to you or not, but that isn't important either. Are you willing to try that? Are you willing to try it really? To work at it? And if you work at it—really work at it, despite all the things that we know about the psychology of relations and all the learned things—if you really work at it, you can depend upon this: that there will open up to you, more and more, the strength to keep on working at it. Not to achieve it—that is beside the point—but that is the assignment of man, and the degree to which he stays in school and works at it, to that degree it is a reasonable thing to dream about a time when this world will be a decent place for friendly men underneath a friendly sky. Let's try it and see.

6

COMMITMENT

Building a Tower/King Going to War
(Luke 14:25-35)

An important context for this 1951 sermon is Thurman's classic work, Jesus and the Disinherited, that had been published in 1949.[1] The message of Jesus was born out of a context of suffering, oppression, and persecution, with the majority of people, including Jesus, living "with their backs constantly against the wall," that is, they were poor, disinherited, underprivileged, and dispossessed (3). Jesus's message was to those people, a message that focused on the urgency of radical change within the individual and, therefore, in society, because the transformation of individuals ultimately leads to a transformation of society.

The position of Jesus as a poor, disinherited Jew in the Roman Empire, is the position of disinherited people in every place and era, so Jesus's message rings true for all people with their "backs against the wall" (12); his message is a guidebook for survival for the oppressed, and Jesus's solution "becomes the word and work of redemption for all the cast-down people in every generation and in every age" (18). The history of Christianity records, however, that Christianity has betrayed the faith of Jesus and has become all too often the religion of the powerful and the dominant, and

---

1. Howard Thurman, *Jesus and the Disinherited* (Boston: Beacon, 1996; originally published by Abingdon Press in 1949).

sometimes Christianity has even become a force that op-
presses other human beings (18-19): "It cannot be denied
that too often the weight of the Christian movement has
been on the side of the strong and the powerful and against
the weak and oppressed—this, despite the Gospel" (20).[2]

In this sermon we catch a glimpse of the brilliance of
Thurman's insights into the life and message of Jesus of
Nazareth, including Thurman's prophetic critique of how
Christianity has lost its way and deviated from the path
envisioned by Jesus. Thurman explores what it means to
be a follower of Jesus, the necessary conditions of being his
disciple, through the lens of two parables: building a tower
and a king going to war.[3]

The two parables have a similar structure: an opening
question, a deliberation over resources for the task at hand,
and an analysis of the expected result should the resources
be insufficient. Both parables indicate that there are costs
involved in being a true follower of Jesus. Following Jesus,
then, involves a deliberate and serious commitment.

Thurman reminds us that Jesus of Nazareth proclaimed a radical and dangerous message. Thurman also
warns us of the pervasive tendency of Christians to domesticate that radical message, to water it down or to ignore
parts of it entirely, so that we can claim to be followers of
Jesus when, in fact, we are not following his call for radical discipleship. Thurman warns us that Jesus says danger-

---

2. The segregation found in churches is one area in which
"American Christianity has betrayed the Religion of Jesus almost beyond redemption" (88).

3. Thurman cites a "British historian" who had argued that the
Greco Roman world "had lost its nerve." This terminology stems from
Gilbert Murray's *Five Stages of Greek Religion* (London: Watts and
Company, 1925). Derived from a series of lectures in 1912 at Columbia
University, Murray's book argues that the "fourth stage" in Greco-
Roman history was "A Failure of Nerve" (123–72).

We have been unable to ascertain the unfinished building in Indianapolis, Indiana, to which Thurman refers in this sermon.

ous things, including sayings that we have tried to make
mean something else entirely, "but it still says that." No
matter how much or how often we attempt to domesticate
Jesus, "he's the most dangerous figure on the horizon of
mortal man" and "Jesus of Nazareth is the greatest enemy
of our civilization and our culture."

Following Jesus of Nazareth thus takes an all-encompassing commitment—the "totality of the personality"—to
the love-ethic of Jesus and its implications for individuals
and for society. Thurman urges us to deliberate over the
costs, to imagine the possibilities, and to respond by saying,
"Here I am."

Commitment

October 21, 1951

SCRIPTURE

And there went great multitudes with him: and he
turned, and said unto them, "If any man come to
me, and hate not his father, and mother, and wife,
and children, and brethren, and sisters, yea, and his
own life also, he cannot be my disciple. And whosoever doth not bear his cross, and come after me, cannot be my disciple. For which of you, intending to
build a tower, sitteth not down first, and counteth
the cost, whether he have sufficient to finish it? Lest
haply, after he hath laid the foundation, and is not
able to finish it, all that behold it begin to mock him,
saying, 'This man began to build, and was not able to
finish.' Or what king, going to make war against another king, sitteth not down first, and consulteth
whether he be able with ten thousand to meet him

that cometh against him with twenty thousand? Or else, while the other is yet a great way off, he sendeth an ambassage, and desireth conditions of peace. So likewise, whosoever he be of you that forsaketh not all that he hath, he cannot be my disciple."

"Salt is good: but if the salt hath lost his savour, wherewith shall it be seasoned? It is neither fit for the land, nor yet for the dunghill; but men cast it out. He that hath ears to hear, let him hear."

—Luke 14:25–35 (KJV)

SERMON

We are thinking together again this morning about certain of the very simple insights from the parables of Jesus, the stories that he told. And today I'd like you to think about the significance of being a disciple in the sense of being fundamentally committed to the religious experience and the religious livingness that dominated and electrified and sustained the life of Jesus. There is a fundamental inspiration in the move—I guess that's the word—that Christianity made in its attack upon the Greco-Roman world, a world that was collapsing, that was disintegrating, that was full of disorder. A world that, as one British historian has described it, a world that had lost its nerve. Men have watched the coming of autumn, the leaves turn golden and red and all sorts of colors, and then they begin to fall off, and the trees are stripped of their leaves, and all the woods become stark and dark and barren. But that does not apply in California [laughter], because in the wintertime, things get green even out here. It's a strange contradiction of life. But that's all right; this is the West. But men have watched that for years, and then winter setting in, and everything tightening, and closing in, and there seems to be no life. All the vitality is at a standstill. And then as the year unfolds, one morning a new odor is in the air, and the back of winter seems to be broken, and there is a strange warmth in the sun. And then underneath the melting snow, the little flowers begin to stir, and then grass, and then the leaves, and before you know it, everything is new again. Now men have been observing that for as long as they have been aware of their environment.

And they have found it a source of very great naturalistic hope for themselves. I've known many people in my lifetime who were ill and who said, "If I can make it through the winter, then, when the renewal of life comes in the spring time, if my organism is not too broken to stand the resurgence of life, I shall live." It's interesting.

Now, what happened when the Christian movement saw this? And when, by some amazingly miraculous insight, inspiration, the central character of their faith, a person was seen as one who in his livingness dramatized this thing that was happening in the world of nature? It's interesting. It's amazing. And when he dramatized it, and they seized upon it, and that became for them the new thing in their faith, the new outreach. So that wherever, in any part of the world, there were people who were depressed, wherever there were people who were distressed, who were disinherited, who were broken on the wheel, what was the word of this religion to them? We talk to you of one who brings to you the tiding that if winter comes, can spring be far behind? That is it. It's an interesting thing, isn't it? But that's not the point.

Now, it is small wonder, then, that at the heart of the teaching is the insistence both upon love and upon sacrifice. A kind of appeal to the commitment of the total life of the individual. Now with that background, let's look at one or two of these parables, and then I'll be through.

Here is a man who started to build a tower. You've seen them in almost every city, haven't you? Every time I go to Indianapolis, I look for that particular set of about eight steel stories, just the buildings, just the steel girders are standing there; it's been standing there for years. Something happened. It was a good plan, apparently, but something gave out. The result is that it's frozen.

If you start to build a house, and if you're wise, if you are sensible, you'll count the cost so that you will know what's involved and then act accordingly. And I have never built a house, but I understand that even when you plan and you know and you get the word from the people who also plan and know, when you get through with the house it has been more expensive than your planning and your thinking indicated. So that when you think and plan, you are apt to be involved. Now what happens if you don't think and plan is disastrous [laughter].

Very simple story. If you are full of ideas, plans, enthusiasms and don't have anything at the center of it, you burn out. That's what he's saying. Simple. Simple. Or if a king is going out to wage war, and if he has ten thousand men, and his enemy has twenty thousand men, the story is that if he doesn't seem to be able to take a calculating risk, he'll sue for peace, says the story. Interesting.

And [Jesus] prefaces these two stories with the fact that if you don't hate your mother, your father, your sister, your brother, if you don't hate them—and we've worked over that, we've tried to make it say something else, but it still says that. And I wonder what would be your interpretation of the meaning of that? It would be very interesting if we could just stop now and have a little discussion. If you don't hate your mother, father, hate all these people, then you have entangling alliances, and you can't be fully committed. Do you believe that? What do you think he's talking about?

Now, does it mean that he's speaking lightly of these commitments? Or is he insisting that there is but one single and completely all-embracing commitment that is worthy of the human spirit? That if I am committed to anything that is merely equal to me, the commitment becomes an indictment. But I must roam with a hungry heart until at last I can lay hold upon that in yielding to which I exhaust myself. And anything less than that is in the realm of tiddlywinks. It's amazing.

And do you wonder why we have a so-called Christian civilization that doesn't bother with Jesus? He's the most dangerous, the most dangerous figure on the horizon of mortal man. And if we seek to reproduce in ourselves the religion which he experienced, we shall destroy our civilization, and there shall be not one stone left on the other. So, what do we do? We pray to him instead. That's easier. We just walk by as they do once a year in the Soviet Union, I'm told, on Lenin's birthday, pass before his bier and pay tribute. Because this is a dangerous man.

Now, I'd like to add just one more little thing, so as not to confuse you from the main insight. It would seem that in this first parable or story there is a word against showing too much enthusiasm. Enthusiasm that does not have at its center a good, hard, understanding mind. And that is a word that falls on very responsive ears in our time, because we are a generation that is afraid of our feelings. We don't like to feel too much, because if you feel, then you're getting emotional, you know, and you can't get emotional, because if you get emotional then you go off half-cocked, you act without understanding, without responsibility.

We delight in thinking that we are intellectuals, that we think our way through life, you know. But do you? But is that true? Give your minds to it for just a minute. Is that true? Or despite all the evidence apparently to the contrary, may it not be true that we feel our way through life? Now the interesting thing in this connection is that wherever the mind or the intellectual process—how to say this— the thinking process is merely committed to an idea or to a proposition or to a way of life, then it is apt to be ineffective if that is the sole basis of the commitment. It is for this reason, I think, that the history of modern dictatorships reveals that among the first people who are captured or who are led captive by the dictator are the people who make up primarily the intellectual community. It is a matter of amazing interest and significance to me that resistance to the dictator, as far as our recent history of the rash of dictators with which we have been inflicted in our civilization over the past decade or two, with reference to that whole group of them, very rarely has there been any fundamental opposition to the inroads which they made upon [people's] minds in an effort to capture the loyalty of the mind and the spirit, very little opposition on the part of the intellectual community. The universities and the colleges [missing] during times of relative tranquility, and when men were thinking great thoughts without too much social implication, provided the machinery, the intellectual ideology that the clever dictator could use and put body into, give it muscle, give it feeling tone, and let it stomp through the land and capture the emotions and the devotions of the masses of the people.

That's amazingly significant to me. And it suggests, you see, that any commitment, and this commitment of which Jesus speaks, must involve the mind, the thinking process, and it must involve the totality of the personality, that's the feeling tone as well. And if it doesn't involve the totality of the personality, then whatever is able to involve the totality of the personality will capture the loyalty of the individual.

Now please do not misunderstand what I am saying or have said. It is no indictment against feelings or an indictment against minds, but when [we] separate them, one from the other, even in theory, we perish; that's all I'm saying.

Now, is there any thing that you know in the world, any dream, any hope, any idea, any commitment that is capable —this morning as you sit here and think about it—is there any thing that is capable of making an exhaustive demand upon your life, so that for its sake you would feel that the greatest tribute you could pay to your own life is to give your life for that thing? Do you know anything that affects you that way? We need not hurry over this part. Think for a moment. Think. Or are you just living in bits, so that this little part of you will go along with that, and this little part of you will go along with that? I mean, you're all scattered so that you are not of one piece with reference to anything. What is it that is capable of making you say: "Here I am, I am, I am?" For better or for worse, and as you say it, having only one regret, and that is that you don't have more of you to give. Now, whatever is capable of doing that for you is your redeemer. For at last, when you have found that, you've found that which is capable to putting meaning into all the little things you do, all the fragmentary manifestations of your life. So that when you must make a decision as to what you shall do, there is only one crucial question: What is the bearing of that decision on this central thing?

Now if there's nothing that affects you in that way … [long pause] … if there's nothing that affects you in that way, you do not know what it means either to be whole or to be committed. That is why when someone like that hits your horizon, and finally gets the focus on your eye, you drop your tools and follow him. That's the genius of the committed man, whether that commitment is to something that is evil or good. When those of us who are not committed have our whole ken disturbed by the swift moving power of one who is completely involved, all of the limitations and inadequacies of our lives begin to be revealed to us, and we want a sense of being of one piece, so that in the living of our lives we will be whole and not a house divided against itself. That's what he's talking about, and that's why, in my judgment, Jesus of Nazareth is the greatest enemy of our civilization and our culture.

7

POSSESSIONS

The Rich Fool
(Luke 12:13-21)

The parable of the rich fool is another one of those texts that Christians over the centuries have tended to domesticate, something that Thurman warned us about in his previous sermon (chapter 6). Interpreters debate many aspects of this parable, including the rich man's competence as a farmer (e.g., why did he tear down his old barns and not just add additional ones?) and whether or not he was an evil person. For those with "their backs against the wall," however, there is no such debate. As Joel Green observes: "Given the subsistence economy of the peasant population surrounding him, this need for increased personal storage space not directly related to his agricultural activity must have seemed odd in the extreme, if not utterly monstrous."[1] In fact, the first-century cultural setting of this parable demands—from the perspective of peasant artisans such as Jesus—that the rich man be seen in a very negative light, as a member of the oppressive elite, even before we hear his condemnation from God.[2]

---

1. Joel B. Green, *The Gospel of Luke* (Grand Rapids, MI: Eerdmans, 1997), 490.

2. For an analysis of this parable that explains these cultural contexts, see David B. Gowler, "The Enthymematic Nature of Parables: A Dialogic Reading of the Parable of the Rich Fool (Luke 12:16–20)," *Review and Expositor* 109 (2012): 199–217.

The draft of a sermon entitled "Poverty and Riches" given by Thurman on January 27, 1957, one in a series on the religion of Jesus, provides additional insights into his earlier sermon given on October 28, 1951, which is found in this chapter. In the 1957 sermon, Thurman begins by noting that the religion of Jesus was God-centered and that there was no area of life or existence that was outside of this divine context. The purpose of God's creation, therefore, was for all of the living creatures of God's creation to "enter into communal relations with each other and with God." That is the purpose of one's life.

Thurman then argues, as he does in his sermon on the Good Samaritan (chapter 5), that human beings attempt to shelter themselves from the impersonal world of nature and the impersonal aspects of the social order. Wealth allows human beings to build buffers that afford some (albeit limited) protection against those forces.

In the 1957 sermon, Thurman then summarizes the parable of the rich fool and the parable of the rich man and Lazarus. He wisely cautions us not to push the correspondences of the parabolic world to the actual world too far: "Don't make the parable walk on six legs; just let it walk on four." He concludes that whatever gifts people have (e.g., including money), if they consider those gifts their own personal property to do with as they please, then those gifts stand between them and full community—fellowship with other human beings and ultimately with God—and that is when all such gifts become evil.

This earlier 1951 sermon, however, focuses only on the parable of the rich fool. After relating the story of the rich fool, Thurman offers three sketches, all of which demonstrate the negative effects that wealth, property, and the desire for more goods can have on human beings and their relationships. As is often the case, Thurman returns to how this drive to protect ourselves from nature or the social order by erecting barriers can damage us, our relationships with others, and our relationship with God. Are we willing and able to put our resources at the service of God and

others instead of ourselves? Are those resources at the serv-
ice of God, or are they in service only for ourselves?
    The questions that Thurman raises in this sermon, and
the answers he gives, can be summarized with one saying
of Jesus: "For where your treasure is, there your heart will
be also" (Luke 12:34).

THE RICH FOOL

October 28, 1951[3]

MEDITATION AND PRAYER

[missing] . . . to be quiet together for a spell, to sit, to think,
to feel our way into each other's joys and sorrows, to surround ourselves with the great sense of collective destiny.
Each one of us has his own cares and burdens, his own
world of involvements and complexities of stresses and
strains of lights and shadows, of heights and depths, of pain
and pleasure, in ways that are commonplace and in ways
that are shocking. No one of us can live unto himself, no
matter how hard he tries. We are so deeply involved in each
other and in others that often it is difficult to determine
where we begin and the other leaves off. And perhaps in
the quietness we may sense the mystery and the wonder
and the magic of our relatedness, and in that relatedness

---

3. Variations on this sermon were presented on numerous occa-
sions, but the original version, it seems, is one that in an abridged and
edited form appeared in a newsletter for the Church for the Fellowship
of All Peoples as well as in the "Marsh Chapel Weekly." The original is
housed in the Howard Thurman Gotlieb Archival Research Center,
Boston University (HGARC).

become aware each after the pattern of his own sensitiveness of the emergence in our midst of the living spirit of
the living God in whom we live and move and have our
being. What we discover here in the quietness may inform
all of the boundless, limitless spread of mankind everywhere to the end that what we do we know must be done
with an eye singled to its bearing upon the least and the
greatest, the wisest and the most foolish, the meanest and
the righteous of all the children of men.

Whisper in our hearts, O God, our Father, the assurance that what we seek when we are most ourselves, thou
seekest. That when we stumble, thou dost stumble. When
we rejoice, thou dost rejoice. O thou redeemer of the
thoughts and the memories and the souls of men, speak
unto us that we may live; breathe through us that we may
live; think through us that we may live. For without thee, O
God, there is nothing, not even we ourselves. This is the
simple quivering of our spirit as we wait in the quietness for
the movement of thyself within us. Amen.

SCRIPTURE READING

> And one of the company said unto him, "Master,
> speak to my brother, that he divide the inheritance
> with me." And he said unto him, "Man, who made
> me a judge or a divider over you?" And he said
> unto them, "Take heed, and beware of covetous-
> ness: for a man's life consisteth not in the abun-
> dance of the things which he possesseth." And he
> spake a parable unto them, saying, "The ground
> of a certain rich man brought forth plentifully:
> And he thought within himself, saying, 'What shall
> I do, because I have no room where to bestow my
> fruits?' And he said, 'This will I do: I will pull down

my barns, and build greater [barns]; and there will I bestow all my fruits and my goods. And I will say to my soul, Soul, thou hast much goods laid up for many years; take thine ease, eat, drink, and be merry.' But God said unto him, 'Thou fool, this night thy soul shall be required of thee: then whose shall those things be, which thou hast provided?' So is he that layeth up treasure for himself, and is not rich toward God."

                              —Luke 12:13–21 (KJV)

Reading

And now I'd like to read a paragraph written by a man from the Middle East, which gives a rather significant commentary on a certain aspect of our life, and I want you to hold this in the background of your minds also:[4]

> You call your thousand material devices "labor-saving machinery," yet you are forever "busy." With the multiplying of your machinery you grow increasingly fatigued, anxious, nervous, dissatisfied. What-

---

4. Abraham Mitrie Rihbany, *Wise Men from the East and Wise Men of the West* (Boston: Houghton Mifflin, 1922), 83. Martin Luther King, Jr. used this passage from Rihbany in *Strength to Love*, which he wrote in 1962 (originally published by Harper and Row in 1963), while he was teaching a course on social philosophy with Samuel W. Williams at Morehouse College. But King used it also in 1954, first, at Dexter Avenue Baptist Church in Montgomery, Alabama, and intermittently thereafter, including in the August 27, 1967, sermon at Chicago's Mount Pisgah Missionary Baptist Church entitled, "Why Jesus Called a Man a Fool." For an analysis of King's 1967 Chicago sermon, see David B. Gowler, *The Parables after Jesus* (Grand Rapids, MI: Baker Academic, 2017), 223–28.

ever you have, you want more; and wherever you
are you want to go somewhere else. You have a machine to dig the raw material for you, a machine to
manufacture [it], a machine to transport [it], a machine to sweep, a machine to dust, a machine to
carry messages, a machine to write, a machine to
talk, a machine to sing, one to play at the theater,
one to sew, and a hundred others to do a hundred
other things for you, and still you are the most nerv-
ously busy people in the world. Your devices are neither time-saving nor soul-saving machinery. They
are so many sharp spurs which urge you to invent
more machinery to do more business.

SERMON

Now, the story that Jesus tells is very simple and very dramatic one. The picture is carefully and skillfully etched: A
man who is doing well, and his farm has produced many
things, more than he can handle and dispose of. And he
says, "I will make room for them"—which is a very sound
way to do it, I suppose—"I will make room so that I may
store all of these things. And then I will stop worrying about
them. I know I am all set for life, and now I will proceed to
enjoy life." And very dramatically Jesus says the man's a fool
because that night he dies. He didn't have a chance to
enjoy anything after all. Would he have been a fool had he
lived in the story? How about that? That's interesting
[laughter]. Maybe he would have had time? Or is there
such a thing as time, for this? It's interesting. Let your
minds play with that—after now; don't run off.
    One of the most impressive memories of my childhood
is the memory of a man who lived in our hometown, a man
from Hartford, Connecticut. I'm from Florida, and my little town in Florida was a famous place for wintering for

people who could not stand the rigors of the North and who were able to do something about it. I had a job raking leaves after school in this man's yard. He had a very large place, and often he would walk out in the yard and talk to me about Hartford, Connecticut; that's where he came from. That's the first time I had ever heard of Hartford, Connecticut, and he was a very important insurance man there. And we developed an interesting friendship—this fine, wealthy, well-to-do man, who found some fellowship in talking with this schoolboy.

One Saturday, I came to work, and he called me from the window, and he said, "Come in, I want to talk with you. I don't think you'd better rake leaves today." And he sat me down. For some hours—I don't know how long, but all the time I should have been outside raking leaves, of course it was all right with me [laughter]—he told me the story of his life. I wondered why he was doing it—of his struggles and his accumulation of his wealth, and his economic security and his power—he talked about it in detail. Then he showed me a telegram that he had received from his son; then he started talking about his son, then about his daughter, and then about his wife. And then he began weeping. And he said—and this is what I remember—he said, "I have spent an entire lifetime doing two things: accumulating wealth and devoting the rest of my energies to concentrating on my children and my wife. I have looked at those two things all my life, and at nothing else. And as I became all set so that I did not have to worry about money, then the energy I had been placing there, I put at the disposal of my children. And now," said he, "they have all gone sour, and I have no choice but to continue concentrating upon them. Do you think a man like me, this late in life, can learn how to develop an interest in people to whom he is not related and to whom he is not obligated?"

My first year in Divinity School—all this has a point, you will see, so just be patient. My first year in Divinity School I had a wonderful Big Ben pocket watch. It had a loud tick, and whenever I went anywhere to speak, a part of the pretensions was to take this watch out and put it up here, you know [on the pulpit], and pulpits were somewhat hollow, and it made a sounding board for the watch, and those who sat near could hear this thing ticking, and I spoke unhurriedly and with a lot of quiet stretches. I wasn't bothered by it, but other people were [laughter]. So a friend of mine gave me a beautiful, thin, white gold Elgin watch that I would have to hold close to my ear in order to hear it tick [laughter]. Before I was given that watch, one night each week I had a study group of men and women who were employed and who were not free from their work until after ten o'clock at night. I walked a couple of miles across town to have this study group; when we'd get through at about 12:30 or 12:45, and I'd walk all the way back, and think nothing of it. But after I had the watch, I was afraid to walk back, lest someone might rob me.

There's one more picture. Tolstoy tells a story about a man who had the richest land in all the Russias. He agreed that any person who came to him and brought all of his personal funds, he would, in exchange for those funds, give to the person bringing the offering all the rich land around which the person could run from sunrise to sunset. You get the picture. So the hero of Tolstoy's tale came and brought his offering and started running. He wished, as he ran along, that he had slept all night so as to have been refreshed for this running, but his mind was harassed, and he was excited and anxious about this rich land, because all of his life he had wanted rich land! The desire had shuttled in and out between all of the dreams of his youth. He kept running, kept running, his feet beating a rhythmic pattern on the soil—rich land, rich land, rich land—until at last he looked up, and he saw that the sun was beginning to dip behind the trees, and he knew that despite his exhaustion, despite all of the weariness of his body, he would have to put forth now the last tremendous effort in order to get back to the starting place before sunset. And he could hardly make it, but he knew he had to make it, because this is it! This is the fulfillment of my dream. Everything else will be possible for me now that I have the rich land, rich land. And when he got back to the place from which he started, Tolstoy says he dropped dead, and they took him aside and buried him six feet under the ground, and that's all the rich soil he could use.

Now I want to ask you two questions, and these questions presuppose a very simple observation that does not require any wisdom. We are human beings living in a society, and we do have the intricate and devastating problem of trying to protect ourselves from the impersonal workings of the world of nature by wearing clothes, by getting houses to protect us from the storm and the weather. We also must protect ourselves from the impersonal operations of the social order by insulating ourselves with barriers of one kind or another that will give to us a quiet moment of retreat in security, that we may stabilize our common life and rear our children, eat, and have some surcease from the impersonal ravages of a ruthless economic order. That's obvious. It is also obvious that we are so involved in the kind of order which is our familiar, that almost unconsciously we measure values in terms of economic units. As one contemporary writer says about a certain man: "His eyes were dollars signs that glowed in the dark." Now we recognize that this is a practical world in which you must have food to eat, and with which you must make some measure of peace in order to survive. Now there are two questions...

If you measured your life in terms of your units of concentration, if your units of concentration could be transposed in terms of values, what would they look like? Let's not hurry over that. What would they look like? Take your day; take your week. Let's think about ourselves, now. Take your week. How much of your energy, time during the past seven days, have you spent involved in things in which you believe? Or has your time been spent getting these things out of the way so that you can have ten minutes to breathe? Or, are you spending your energy and your time working on behalf of those things? What about it? Or do you say to me: "If I had all of my other problems solved, then, of course, it would be a reasonable thing to assume that I could give my mind and thought over to these luxuries of the spirit or luxuries of the mind." Is that the way you feel? That so much of your energy and time must be spent, for instance, in the ordinary crass business of earning a living, guaranteeing your protection against either one or the other or both of these impersonal forces about which I spoke a moment ago. And therefore it is not a reasonable thing to assume that you can give your time and thought to something else. What about it?

Now the second question: How much detachment do you practice with reference to the things that encumber your life? How much of you do you put at the disposal of trying to work out the problem of your involvement? What is your fundamental attitude toward money, for instance? Is it an instrumentality by which you communicate and make active your will to dominate and control your fellows? This is a perfectly good question to ask. Now you can do that, you see, not merely if you are a person of great and vast economic power.

I remember that when I had my little church in Oberlin, Ohio, when I was in Divinity School, we wanted to send one of our boys to a high school conference down in North Carolina. I asked all the high school girls and boys if they would join me in selling to the community whole boxes of Schrafft's candy. They urged churches to do that, where you would pay eighty cents or some amount for the candy and sell it for a dollar and twenty cents. These girls and boys agreed to do it. They were quite excited about it, because one of their fellows was going to go down to North

Carolina and attend this conference. And I came into the young people's meeting one Sunday afternoon, and they had decided *to take the place apart.* They were just high school people enjoying themselves, oblivious to where they were. They did everything except take the pews up with screwdrivers. When I walked in, my first impulse was to do what I finally did do—but—but at first I froze that impulse, because along with the impulse came another idea—you'd better be careful! Because you have paid $42.00 for all that candy, and these youngsters have agreed to sell it, and you are to give it to them tonight! Now if you offend them, even though they are completely in error here, then they will not sell the candy, and if they don't sell the candy, then you are out of the money, and this boy, Hoffman, will not be able to go to the conference down in North Carolina. All that went through my mind in a split second. So I told them what I thought of them, and did it perhaps with much more intensity because of my own inner battle, you see, than I would have had if I had no struggle going on. And they agreed that I would sell my own candy [laughter]. I waited, and I think that one of the things life teaches you more and more is to learn how to wait. You can—if you just wait and don't run a temperature—sit it out. About Wednesday they came around. That's very crude, but we're *always* tempted to do that with even a little bit of economic power. If this doesn't go well, then how shall I express my feeling about it? I shall withdraw my economic support! Simple; and that is, or may be, another way of saying that my economic support must be alongside and on behalf of the thing to which I am committed and in which I believe. Now my behavior may be of that kind if that is my position, but most often it is, if my will is thwarted, then I use my economic support on behalf of judgment and punishment for those who fought my will.

How are you related to your money? How are you related to it? And it is no answer to say that you don't have any. That's no answer. How are you related to your money? Is it a part of your commitment to God, or is it a part merely of your commitment to yourself? That's the crucial question. If I give all of my life goods to support causes in which I do not believe, or if I withhold the bowels of my generosity and compassion from the need that always hammers at my door, then I will never find freedom of mind, of spirit, of heart. Therefore, Jesus raises with awful insistence: *What would I give in exchange for my life?* Do I give my money, my things? Am I so attached to them that to detach myself from them is equivalent to destroying myself? Or is it possible for me to put at the disposal of [others] the fruits of my labor, bearing in mind that everything that I have, I have because of a lot of other people's work, a lot of other people's labor, a lot of other people's sacrifice, a lot of other people's self-denial? It's the most stupid thing in the world for a man to say, "I did this myself." He didn't.

Now, are you willing—and I'm through now—are you willing to put the resources of your mind at the disposal of trying to work out the most creative way by which you can live your life, placing your possessions at the disposal of that to which you are committed? And the degree to which you are able to do that, you will find peace of mind and freedom of soul.

What about it? Are you willing to try it? See what happens.

8

THE LOST

The Lost Sheep and the Lost Coin
(Luke 15:4–10)

Thurman delivered this lecture in his 1957 "Religion of Jesus" series almost six years after his 1951 sermons on the Lost Sheep, Lost Coin, and Lost (Prodigal) Son in chapters 2 and 3 of this volume. The key message (which, in Thurman's view, has not changed) of these parables is the critical importance of community with God and with each other.

This community, divine and human, stems from the fact that God is the creator and sustainer of all things and that the divine purpose is that "there shall be increasingly in all creation, community, a sense of ingatheredness, a sense of wholeness, a sense of integration." For that reason, because we are God's creatures, human beings desire and hunger for this sense of community above all else.

We are lost without that community, as the "simple story" of the lost sheep brilliantly illustrates. Like human beings, the lost sheep, in Thurman's imagination, becomes (self-) absorbed in other things and becomes isolated from others and "from the center around which his life revolved." For human beings this separation includes isolation from the deeper meaning of life and from God. Or, as the parable of the lost coin illustrates, sometimes this isolation occurs because of circumstances beyond one's con-

trol, as in the heartbreaking story of the "untouchable" boy Thurman encountered in India (in 1935-36).[1]

In both the parable of the lost sheep and in the parable of the lost coin, the "lostness" is non-deliberate. The prodigal son parable, however, illustrates a third aspect of human lostness: sometimes people deliberately decide to isolate themselves from others and from God and, hopefully like the prodigal son, they will "come to themselves" and realize that God is their father. Since they are God's children, they have God's "mark" of God's creation in them, that "sensitive, palpitating, quivering divine dimension of us that is always seeking to align, to get into harmony, to complete the cycle" between them and God.

As a consequence, the movement toward God is a shared initiative: Human beings can "come to themselves," but there always is "the persistent pull of God" leading us to re-establish our community with God and therefore with others. God does not rest—in fact, "God can never be happy"—until all human beings are in community with God and with all other "living things." Likewise, Thurman argues, we should actively seek to meet the needs of other human beings to make it more likely that they also will be re-established in God's community. Inner salvation necessarily leads to external actions.

---

1. The young boy asked Thurman, "Tell me, please, can you give hope to a nobody?" and fell to his knees. As Thurman tried to lift him up, the boy turned and ran away, and Thurman did not have the opportunity to answer his question: that "within us all is a Presence to which we are responsible," which gives everyone "an immunity against the isolation with which life has fenced us in": Elizabeth Yates, *Howard Thurman: Portrait of a Dreamer* (New York: John Day, 1964), 100–103.

The Lost

January 13, 1957

Meditation

The story of our lives is the old story of man. The need to separate ourselves from the tasks by which our days are surrounded. The urgency within us for some measure of detachment from the traffic and the perplexities of our involvement. The anxiety that is within us because there seems to be so little time for withdrawal and reflection. All of these crowd in upon us to fill our minds as we wait in the presence of God and in the midst of our congregation or our homes. It is not easy to spread our lives out even before us, but this we understand as we wait in the quietness. The obvious things in our lives we pass over, taking them for granted, which in fact may be a source of our weakness and despair. We are aware of limitations in some dimensions in our lives. We are conscious of the ways in which and by which we have undermined the light of the truth that is within us. There are things in our lives at which we have not looked for a long time. We lift them out and spread them gently before God. There are some things within us that are so far beneath the surface of our movements and our functioning that we are unmindful not only of their presence but also of the quality of their influence on our decisions, judgment, and behavior. We will in the quietness to expose those to God with the hope that we may become aware of them ourselves and that they may be lifted to the center of our focus that we may know what they are and seek to do with them that which is in keeping with our health and our wisdom.

All of the involvements of our lives in family, in primary community relations, in our state and country; in our world, the far-flung reaches of the things that we affect and the things that affect us. All of the concern that, when we are most ourselves, we have for various aspects of these things which affect us and the things which we affect. All of this we spread before our own eyes and before the scrutiny of God.

We turn to thee, our Father, not out of a sense of worth or lack of worth, not out of a sense of pride or lack of pride, but we turn to thee with our total life because this seems to speak directly to our deepest need. What thou seest in us that is weak and unworthy of our best, wilt thou handle in thine own way. What thou seest in us that is strong and vital, wilt thou encompass in thine own way. We yield as best we can everything, everything, our Father, holding back nothing, and we wait for thy benediction and thy healing. We wait, O God, God, our Father, in the quietness.

SERMON

We have been saying now for many weeks that the religion of Jesus is God-centered, that to Jesus God was the creator of life and of the living substance; he was the creator of existence itself, and that there is no thing that is outside the divine context, that all life is involved in the creative activity of God, the creator, and that fundamental to life is the divine purpose, and the divine purpose is that there shall be increasingly, in all creation, community, a sense of ingatheredness, a sense of wholeness, a sense of integration. If I could lay bare that which above all else I desire, that which above all else I hunger for, it would be precisely that which is the purpose of God.

Now, a man is lost when he is out of community, when he has a sense of being isolated, cut off from his immediate direct conscious involvement in the collective destiny of life and man. The sinner, then, is one who is out of community. This seems to me to be fundamental to the teachings of Jesus, and fundamental to his religious insight and his religious experience. He expressed this in at least three very simple but meaningful and significant parables. It is apart from my purpose to go into these in detail, but let us look. First, the man who is lost, who is out of community because of the pursuit of ends which...become for him increasingly private, personal, and self-centered. In the realization of these ends, in the full-orbed fulfillment of these ends, the net result is that he is cut off, isolated from his fellows, from the deeper meaning of his life, from God. And Jesus sketched this in the simple story of the lost sheep. The sheep that was enjoying his grass and delighting itself in all of its possibilities. So absorbed was he in this that he was not even aware of the fact that the sun was going down, nor of the fact that the sun had gone down, nor was he aware of the fact that there wasn't anybody else there except him. Now, of course, it is right for the sheep to eat the grass. He was doing a perfectly natural, normal thing. But when this perfectly natural, normal thing became the all-consuming end of his life, when to get his stomach full dominated his horizon and became the center around which his life revolved—when that happened, he was lost. Whenever a man reduces all of life to a single dimension and lets this dimension become the center around which all of the grounds of his integration move, he is thrown out of relationships, even though the thing may be a good thing within itself. He is found, he is saved, he once again has a sense of wholeness when this particular thing is placed in proper and definitive perspective and meaning.

Second, a man is lost when he experiences isolation, out of community because of a set of circumstances or conditions over which he is unable to exercise and immediate control, and says to himself that he will accept as the total answer and meaning to his life the event which holds him prisoner. It may be that the door to community was closed as a result of some upheaval that took place in his world over which he had no control. The simple words that we use to describe it are "he is a victim of circumstances." The circumstances may be that which is defined in bills of lading, for instance, as "an act of God." He is lost when he accepts the fact as the be-all and end-all of life that the event that holds his life in its agonizing grapple is his prison house. It may be disease, it may be the victims of war, it may be the little children who are orphaned, or the refugees in the camps, in different parts of the world, those whose experience has seen the door to community close in their face, and they relax their inner pressure on holding the door open. They are found, they are redeemed, when the door to community is open.

I remember twenty years ago when I was in India, one night about 9:30, after I had retired, I heard someone knocking gently on the door. I got up and went to the door, and here was a boy. When I spoke to him, he did not lift up his head, it remained bowed in a sort of abjectness. He said, "I stood outside listening to your talk tonight. I am an untouchable. I am a nobody. I wonder if there is anything that can be said or done that can help me." Lost. Every time you feel that way, you are lost too.

Now, the third, and then I will pull these together. The story that Jesus used to illustrate the second [type of lostness] is the story of the lost coin. A new dimension enters into the meaning now. The first two [cases involved] a level that was non-deliberate. Now [in the third type] the man is lost who decides that he will elect to separate himself from community. A full-orbed clearly defined choice on his part. This is the story of the prodigal son who decided that he would leave home. He does and has an experience far away, and then after life had stripped him—and it's very interesting the ways by which we are stripped. Sometimes we do it deliberately in trying to lay bare our lives to God. Other times the relentless pressure and the relentless logic of the events by which our lives are surrounded, these things strip us. This boy was stripped to that which within him was literal and irreducible, as he sat munching the food that had been given to the hogs. Jesus says that he came to himself. He discovered that which was deepest in him, that which he most fundamentally desired over all else, now that the shouting and the tumult had died [and this] was precisely what God wanted. I am my father's son, and my father is my father. When he became aware of this, salvation became operative.

Now all of this is to say that because God is the creator of life, God is the creator of all living things, God is our creator, there is within us the mark of his creation. This sensitive, palpitating, quivering divine dimension of us that is always seeking to align, to get into harmony, to complete the cycle between itself and God. This means that the initiative in salvation—and this is the heart of [what] Jesus is insisting upon—does not merely rest with the repentant sinner, with the man who becomes aware of the fact that he is lost, and as a result of that awareness undertakes to do something about it, but always there is the persistent pull of God who shares the initiative and who often captures the initiative; and every time there is a stirring in my heart that moves me to do the kind deed, the good deed; every time there is the movement within me to right a wrong thing; every time there is an increasing area of sensitiveness that becomes the basis of my communication with my fellows so as to enlarge my sense of community; every time [that] as the result of the impact of my life upon another, there is a stirring within that other person that puts pressure upon the door from the inside of that person to keep the door open, to get a crack in the door so as to re-establish a lost harmony, to re-establish a community, to give to him or to me a sense of being involved in the living of life, in a collective destiny that includes all mankind. Every time I do this, the work of salvation is in me, and if I am inspired so to get equipment or a tool or a skill that will operate upon the lives of other people in meeting their needs, so that it will be increasingly reasonable for them to open the door because their handicaps have been lifted, their diseases have been healed, the fever in their mind has been quieted. Or their sense of loneliness has been broken because now they enter into a dimension of community with another soul, and they seem to themselves now to be of infinite worth when this happens. The morning stars sing together, and the sons of God shout for joy, and the loneliness of God because one of his creatures is out of community is broken. God can never be God to his creation if there is a single expression of his creation that is out of harmony. For better or for worse, God and I, God and you, are bound together, and I cannot be what it is that I must be if between you and me, between you and God, there is no community. However far ahead of himself the turtle puts his two front feet, he can't move his body until he moves his hind legs. For better or for worse, the redemption of the whole creation rests upon the redemption of a single human being. God cannot be happy in his heaven if any man is in hell. Therefore, I must work out my salvation by seeking in every way to further communion between myself and all living things and myself and God. Who am I that with my life and my limitations, my sins, my bigotry, who am I that I should hold up the work of salvation in the world and beyond? God is the God of the lost and the found. For he is the God of all of life. This is my strength and my repentance.

BENEDICTION

Forgive our sins O Father, all the ways by which we rupture community and bring sadness and loneliness to thy heart. Walk with us as we seek community, and when we stray, let us hear thy voice and feel thy sustaining arms around us. Dismiss us with thy Spirit and grant unto us thy peace.

9

THE JUDGMENT

The Sheep and Goats
(Matthew 25:31-46)

This sermon is another installment in the "Religion of Jesus" series Thurman delivered at Boston University's Marsh Chapel in 1957. It contains some of the essential components of Thurman's theology, including the key element of why one's faith should lead to social action, and Thurman uses the parable of the sheep and goats in Matthew 25 as his scriptural touchstone.

The opening meditation foreshadows Thurman's arguments in the body of the sermon: his prayer—actually, he would argue, the prayer of the community gathered that day which he is led to utter—is for people in contemporary society, many of whom could be included in the parable's "least of these"—such as the lonely, homeless, and confused. Thurman prays that the wisdom, understanding, and judgment of God will "evolve in us and in them that will make thy kingdom effective, dominant, and real..." This kingdom can emerge, however, only when people offer themselves completely to God. Then God will work through them, and God's kingdom will come (as in the Lord's Prayer, Matthew 6:10).

Thurman's account of how one's religious experience should necessarily lead to social action can be compared to other expressions of faith-in-action. The Epistle of James, for example, declares: "faith without works is dead."[1] Yet Thurman could have drawn on similar perspectives in other religions, such as the idea found in Hinduism that selfless devotion-in-action to God can lead to liberation.[2]

Thurman begins by placing the concept of the kingdom of God in its first-century contexts, such as the hope proclaimed by Hebrew prophets that God would establish through Israel "a sovereignty inclusive of the entire human race" or the apocalyptic belief by others that God would invade human history precipitously. Jesus's pronouncement of the kingdom of God in these contexts means that individuals are responsible agents who are under obligation to yield their "centers" to God and to the will of God so that "right" actions will flow from that center in "right relationships" with God and other human beings.

But, as Thurman recognizes, although individuals are responsible agents, they are responsible to a larger group and thus are limited and bound by that community.[3] Thurman balances the responsibility of the individual (we take part in the "writing" of our lives) with one's responsibility to the group, a responsibility that individuals recog-

---

1. James 2:14–17: "What good is it, my brothers and sisters, if you say you have faith but do not have works? Can faith save you? If a brother or sister is naked and lacks daily food, and one of you says to them, 'Go in peace; keep warm and eat your fill,' and yet you do not supply their bodily needs, what is the good of that? So faith by itself, if it has no works, is dead."

2. Devotion-in-action, for example, is a recurrent theme in the Bhagavad Gita (e.g., 3:9; 5:2; 9:26–27; 11:51–55).

3. Thurman alludes to the story of Achan in Joshua 7 when he uses the "no pillaging" example to explain one's responsibilities to the group. The Israelites were commanded by God not to take plunder from the destruction of Jericho (Joshua 6:18–19). Achan did, however (7:1, 18–21), take plunder and, as a result of his disobedience, about thirty-six Israelites were killed by the people of the city of Ai (7:5). As punishment for his disobedience, Achan, his entire family, and all his possessions were destroyed (7:22–26).

nize once they refer their "deeds to the center." Thurman argues that Jesus's "very moving picture" of the Last Judgment in his parable of the sheep and goats illustrates this relationship.[4] *If one refers one's deeds to the center, one inherently recognizes the critical importance of visiting the sick, ministering to those in prison, feeding the hungry, and clothing the naked. Therefore, human beings are not merely responsible to themselves, but they also are not merely responsible to their group or even to the larger society: Human beings are responsible to God for what they do, and what they decide determines whether they go to the "left" or to the "right."*

THE JUDGMENT

February 17, 1957

MEDITATION

We bring before our thoughts and the focusing of our minds and spirits in a special manner cradled in tenderness, concern, and imagination all the students of the world and their needs. The students in refugee camps, and the vast uncertainty by which their moments are surrounded. The students in Egypt, Israel, South Africa, and particularly the students of the College of [missing]. The students of Hungary. The students in our own land. The grade school students, the

---

4. This apocalyptic parable seems to assume the pattern in Palestine of maintaining a mixed herd of sheep and goats. The apocalyptic elements include the judgment where they are separated, similar to the parable of the wheat and weeds (Matthew 13:24–30) in the sermon in chapter 1 of this book.

high school students in the southland whose lives are caught in the great squeeze play of social forces that daze and bewilder and confuse.[5] The students of our own university. The lonely ones, the homeless ones, the aimless ones, the confused ones, the dedicated ones—all of these crowd in upon our sights, each with the claim of that which is deepest within him crying out for fulfillment. We hold ourselves and them steadily, quietly, with great concentration before thy altar, our Father. Invade their lives, their contexts, their surroundings, not only with thy wisdom and thy understanding, but with thy judgment and its vitality to the end that something will evolve in us and in them that they will make thy kingdom effective, dominant, real in the way that we take. We do not ask. We do not plead. We do not beg. We offer them and ourselves, and we wait, we wait, O God, in thy presence. We wait; thou wilt not reject our spirits, our Father.

SERMON

We continue our thinking together about the religion of Jesus and the significance of the kingdom of God within

---

5. Thurman is most likely referring, for example, to the 1956 Suez Crisis; the "Treason Trial" in South Africa, where Nelson Mandela and 155 others were put on trial in South Africa for treason; the Hungarian Revolution of 1956 against the Hungarian government, which was controlled by the USSR; and, most likely, the forthcoming integration of public schools in Little Rock, Arkansas, and other places. In September, 1957, Arkansas Governor Orval Faubus, even after the Supreme Court's 1954 *Brown v. Board of Education* decision, ordered the Arkansas National Guard to prevent nine African-American students (the "little Rock Nine") from entering the all-white Little Rock Central High School in Little Rock. The students were finally enrolled after the mayor of Little Rock asked President Dwight Eisenhower to intervene.

the context of his religious insight and his religious experience. It is important to [remember] that the kingdom of God in the experience of Jesus has at its roots the ancient hope of Israel, this dream that there would come a time in the life of man when God would actively take possession and control of the life of his chosen, and through them establish a sovereignty inclusive of the entire human race. The prophets felt that this dream was being worked out in the creative movement of human history. There were others who felt that man had become so degenerate and evil, and society so full of stain and war and sin and madness that God had withdrawn from man and left man to work out his evil designs within the movement of a relentless logic, but [that] there would come a time when, as a result of a precipitous movement of God invading human history, the age would end and all of the contamination would be wiped out and the new era would be brought in by this apocalyptic movement of God—outside of human history but making contact with history by a precipitous invasion—[and so the new era] would be realized. This is the root. God is the creator of life and the living substance. God is the creator of existence; therefore everything...lives under God. The logic of this is [that] the individual lives as a responsible agent, and he is under obligation to let his life flow out from his center. [This] center has at its core the yielding of the nerve center of consent to the will of God, so that the action that flows out from this center that is always accessible to the will of God will be right action, the relationship will be right relationship. When Jesus announces that the kingdom of God is at hand, this is the announcement that he is making.

[For[those who have exposed themselves to the invasion, to the will, to the love of God and have yielded to him the centrality of [their] focus and purpose and motivation and life, the actions that flow out of that center are right

actions, and the relationships are right relationships. If all
the human beings in the world are thus conditioned, are
thus dedicated, then the actions of the men in the world
will be an expression of the will of God in the world, but
the responsibility of the individual remains always the
same. He is responsible for his actions. First, in the development of this concept, he is responsible to the group for
his actions. Those of us who are acquainted with the background of the religion out of which Jesus came recognize
at once [the importance of] this concept of the group and
the way the individual was related to the group. He was responsible to the group. He held in his decisions, decisions
that were never private, but always involved the group. In
battle, if a man were told that there should be no pillaging
in the conquest, and if a man, as is recorded in the Old
Testament, decided that this is a beautiful something, this
is too pretty to be left here to the weather, to the elements;
I think my family can use this, or my friend, or my wife.
[And so] he stuck it under his saddle out of sight, and because this individual had done this the whole group had
been contaminated and suffered. The responsibility of the
individual for his action, but this responsibility is limited
and bounded by the group.

Then, the development moves a little further. An individual is not merely responsible for his own actions and to
the group of which he is a part whose etiquette and whose
values are his, but he is responsible to a wider relationship;
he is responsible to the society.

Now, in modern psychology we come to an interpretation of the individual as being responsible for his own actions and responsible to himself. Everything that he does
registers in his own life. Nothing walks with aimless feet. A
man is at any particular moment in his life the result of an
infinite series of yesterdays; he cannot isolate a single moment or any deed of his from the total pattern of his life.

He is always involved in the story he is writing. It is curious how this concept of judgment, the judgment that life passes upon the individual for what he does, is dramatized in this very moving picture that Jesus gives of the end of the age, the time when the Judge is seated on his throne. Time is no more. All the people are gathered before the throne. The sheep on the right, the goats on the left. It is automatic:

> "I was sick, and you did not come to see me. I was in I was in prison, and you did not administer to my need there. I was hungry, and you let me starve. I was naked, and you would not restore my self-respect by giving me clothes to wear. This you did. Therefore, you go to the left."

> "But I didn't know that it was that important. For some reason, I was so involved in the living of my life, in handling my own affairs, in doing my thing, that I did not refer my deeds to my center. I referred my deeds to some other aspect of my life. To my anxieties, it is out of these that I acted. It is out of my fears that I acted. It is out of my ambitions that I acted. It is out of my pride that I acted, always getting my clue as to what I should do from something less than my center. Something less than that which is at the core of me."

The Judge says that a man is not merely responsible to the group by which his life gets its meaning and identification, the primary group [in] which he becomes a person. He is not merely responsible to the society that gives to him certain overarching guarantees with reference to which he may have some measure of emotional and mental stability. He is not merely responsible to himself and the kind of human being that his deeds will create, but he is responsible to God. Ultimately, a man is responsible to God for what he does. The history of a man's life is his judgment. The deeds that the men did determined it. My deed sent me here. My deed sent me there.

When your life moves out of a center which has been yielded to the will and to the spirit and to the determination of God, you become a very interesting kind of person. You become kind and gracious. When your deeds move out of that which is central in you, then you do what you are when you are most yourself, you know that if this were done to you, it would [make] all the difference in how you felt. It is an interesting commentary on our kind of society, the kind of lives that we live. This is so commonplace, I am almost embarrassed to talk about it. When we encounter a kind person, a gracious person, and [aren't] related to that person in some way, we become suspicious. It's amazing. The abnormal individual is a person who is kind and gracious. You wonder what is up, what he is preparing you for. When will the bite come?

Two years ago when we were visiting Denison University in Ohio, as we walked around campus everybody who passed us, whether they were students or professors, everybody spoke to us with a smile, and we wondered where we were. Commenting upon it as we were driving back from Denison to Columbus, we were trying to wrap our thoughts and minds around this that we had experienced as something that was normal. We know that it belonged to our peace, but to accept it meant to honor it in what we did. This is a little more difficult.

When I was a boy I was always contemplating Thanksgiving, because Thanksgiving was the last milestone before Christmas, and Christmas meant a very special thing. After Thanksgiving I began moving out of a certain kind of center. I was a good boy. My mother did not ever have to ask me twice to do anything. I could anticipate her needs. I had a sense of what was vital. I drew on everything that I knew about her so that I couldn't miss, because I knew that Christmas was coming and that if I had surrounded her with all of the graciousness and sensitiveness and thoughtfulness, [then]out of the goodness of her heart, she would know that I had become a different kind of boy, and she would encourage me effectively on Christmas morning. Now, this is very naïve. But what life is like in the kingdom of God in the thought of Jesus is this. My right deed, my right relationship, my right action move out of a center of that kind, and it is not my responsibility if the individual to whom it moves rejects it, abuses it, flings it back in my teeth. My responsibility is to let my action and my relationships move out of this center. How many times shall I forgive? Seventy times? Seventy times seven? My forgiveness has nothing to do with whether the individual merits it or doesn't merit it, whether he will think that I am soft and a pushover or not. My responsibility to God is to let my action and the context and motivation of my relationships move out of this center, for every man is responsible to God for his life and for what he does. Therefore, I shall not make of myself an instrument to punish men for their deeds. Judgment belongs to God. My judgment, yours. So if in how I relate to you I become the instrument of God's judgment, I am acting out of character, for the moment I do that, I become involved in the very thing in me that I am resisting in you. The kingdom of God means that at the center of my life, at the nerve center of my consent, I affirm the priority of God in my life, and I manifest this sense of his priority in my actions and in how I relate to other people. The responsibility for how other people relate to me is not mine. This is a very insane way to run the world, but until the world is run this way, the world will be an insane world, and wherever a man does this, there at that moment the kingdom of God is at hand. Can you bring yourself to make such a decision? Can you? Will you try it and see?

BENEDICTION

Dismiss us, O God, with thy Spirit and leave us not alone in the grip of so much that destroys and depresses. Deliver us from evil as we seek to do thy will, thy will, O God. Thy will.

10

THE GREAT FEAST

(Luke 14:12-24)

This sermon is the third of four sermons in this volume from Thurman's 1957 "Religion of Jesus" series, and the keys to understanding it are found in the two parts of the opening meditation. The first stresses that God, no matter the outward circumstances, is always beside us, within us, and, paradoxically, "with, in, and among the struggling elements of my own experience." The second, connected to and perhaps dependent in some ways on the first, is that we should strive to do what is good not because of some promised reward either in this life or the next but because it is good.

The focus in this sermon is again on Jesus's proclamation and understanding of the kingdom of God in the context of his religious experience and resulting vision of God. In essence, it is the surrendering to God of what is most central to one's existence. Thurman believes that once such surrendering occurs, then the kingdom of God can operate within and through that person. The result is not only right actions but also right relationships.

Thurman captures the essence of the story in Luke 14 without delving into exegetical details, what he calls "many technical interpretations." Some additional reflections on the text, however, will serve to demonstrate how Thurman builds his interpretation and applications in this sermon on a solid exegetical foundation.

Luke 14:1-24 is the third scene in Luke where Jesus dines in the house of a Pharisee (see 7:36-50; 11:37-54) and the fourth time he heals on the Sabbath (see 4:31-37; 6:6-11; 13:10-17); each time a controversy erupts that serves to clarify Jesus's view of God and human relationships. This particular story in Luke merges and concludes these two Lukan type-scenes, and it begins ominously by noting that those attending the banquet "were watching [Jesus] closely"; their opposition to Jesus has increased in the course of Luke's Gospel. Since the dinner was on the Sabbath, which had been a particular focus of their previous debates (e.g., Luke 6:1-5 and 6:6-11), controversy erupted after Jesus healed a man with dropsy (Luke 14:4).

Thurman notes that the great dinner in the parable involves a wealthy host who is concerned about his prestige, so he invites "all the prestige-bearing people in his world" to his great feast. His invited guests spurn him in a way that appears to be planned. He thereby loses prestige and honor, and then he invites all of the disadvantaged he can find to his feast, since his "food will not taste right if there is any man within reach who is hungry."

The Lukan context for this parable reinforces Thurman's observations, since Luke portrays this dinner as taking place in the house of a Pharisee who is a "ruler" 14:1), and the dinner also involves wealthy elite who are problematically concerned about prestige and money (e.g. Luke 11:39-40, 43; 14:7-14; 16:13-14). Luke, in fact, portrays many Pharisees as self-aggrandizing and rapacious, although, as Thurman notes in his sermon on forgiveness (chapter 4 in this volume), that characterization does not fit the historical Pharisees.

Even the healing of the man with dropsy evokes images of greed both for money and prestige, because, in Jesus's time dropsy was an almost proverbial metaphor for greed, since the symptoms of greed parallel those of dropsy. When people suffer from dropsy (edema), their bodies fill with fluid, but, paradoxically, one of the symptoms can be great thirst, even with the excess of fluid in the body. Similarly,

when people accumulate wealth, their greediness—and lack
of empathy for others—often accelerates, even though they
already have great wealth. In this context, then, the man
with dropsy, whose body is filled with fluid but who still
feels great thirst, symbolizes those people present at the
dinner (and among the readers of Luke) who are already
wealthy but are still rapacious and avaricious in spite—or
even because—of that wealth.[1]

The parable offers an example of "conversion" that Jesus
proclaims his host should emulate. What is surprising in
the parable is that the invited guests, who had already accepted the host's invitation to a great banquet, refuse the
host's final summons to dinner with rather questionable
excuses (as Thurman notes, it is "curious" that a man
would buy a pair of oxen before examining them). The
parable thus portrays a deliberate, grievous shaming of the
host by his wealthy elite friends, and the host's reaction—
the repeated invitations to the poor, the maimed, the blind,
the lame, and other marginalized people—is exactly the
type of conversion Jesus seeks: the "haves" reaching out in
fellowship and community to the "have nots." That is how
people treat each other in God's kingdom, and the reason
for these invitations is not because of some reward; it is because it is good; like God is good.[2]

We are all invited to the great feast of God, Thurman
says, and by exposing the deepest hungers of ourselves to
God, we may indeed enter the community of God's great
feast.

---

1. See Willi Braun, Feasting and Social Rhetoric in Luke 14 (Cambridge: Cambridge University Press, 1995), 30–42.

2. Jesus demands that the elite such as this ruler operate with
vertical generalized reciprocity—a redistribution from the advantaged
to the disadvantaged that expects nothing in return. Since God showers humankind with vertical generalized reciprocity, humankind
should follow God's lead in their relationships with each other (e.g.,
11:11–14). See David B. Gowler, Host, Guest, Enemy, and Friend: Portraits
of the Pharisees in Luke and Acts, (Eugene, OR: Wipf & Stock, 2007).

THE GREAT FEAST

February 24, 1957

MEDITATION

"If thou standest beside me nothing can prevail against me." There are times when the sense of aloneness is very acute. Often these are times of struggle where the odds are uneven. Curious indeed is it that the sense of not being alone is apt to be most acutely felt when the concentration upon the matter at hand is absorbing. This means that there is available at the moment no margin of me exposed to the presence of God. To be aware that God is standing beside me calls for some measure of detachment from my own personal struggle and my own personal turmoil. "If thou standest beside me" it is entirely possible that the presence of God may be most acutely felt in and through the struggle and the turmoil. It is not something apart from my involvements but a quality of presence that emerges from the midst of my tempests, or, more accurately, it becomes a quality of the tempest itself. Sometimes this identification becomes very confusing, causing me to say that God brings the struggle. It is sufficient for me to know that he is found in the midst of all that befalls me. Nothing can prevail against me. The affirmation is the result of the disclosure of the presence of God in the midst of that which befalls me. First, he is felt as being with, in, and among the struggling elements of my own experience. Then, out of the midst of these, his presence emerges and [God] becomes one who stands by my side. It is then that I am lifted up and strengthened. "If thou standest beside me, nothing can prevail against me."

READING

> Shall I be good because of some reward,
> Because the virtuous act pays dividends?
> —Kenneth Boulding, "Shall I Be Good?"

The sentence from one of the Nayler sonnets[3] recalls a familiar aspect of our common experience. It is very difficult to escape the searching tyranny of reward and punishment. From early childhood we are drilled in the experience of expecting to be rewarded because we are good and punished because we are bad. Again and again, to be good means to us to be approved. If the act is approved by those who rate highly with us, then it is apt to be regarded as a good act or a good deed. Under such circumstances, the basis of our morality is located outside ourselves completely and is resident in those persons or that person whose esteem we seek and must have, or we are insecure. It is but a simple step from this attitude to the one which ascribes the role of Recorder and Punisher to God. It is most subtle. We may regard ourselves as being free souls, emancipated from superstitions and even religion, and yet there persists in the background of our lives the insistent feeling that our ill fortune is the result of wrong things that we have done. Indeed, this may be true. There is a wide area of human experience in which we are involved directly in the category of reaping and sowing. We cannot escape the logic of this part of the moral law. Individuals as well as nations do reap what they sow. But there is more involved in our central question than this. It is not enough to be good because of some reward, because the virtuous act pays dividends.

---

3. The Nayler sonnets, written by Kenneth Boulding and first published in 1945, are based on the famous final words of James Nayler, an early Quaker who died in 1660.

The virtuous act may or may not pay dividends. In the last analysis, men cannot be persuaded to be good because of the reward either here or beyond this "vale of tears." Men must finally come to the place in their maturity which makes them do the good thing because *it is good*. Not because it is a command, not even because it is a divine command, but because the good deed, the good thought, the good life is *in itself good*. This is the strength of the good deed—that it is good. When this is our awareness, then the whole matter of reward and punishment, approval and disapproval, becomes strangely irrelevant.

> Shall I be good because of some reward,
> Because the virtuous act pays dividends?

No! I shall be good because it is *good*.[4]

SERMON

We are drawing almost to an end of a journey on which we have been going for a long time, and I'm sure you are in need of a change of scenery, but nevertheless it is important to do this. We have been thinking as you know for many weeks about the religion of Jesus, and we are dealing now with certain aspects of his interpretation of the kingdom of God within the context of his religious experience and his vision of God. It has been suggested that to him the individual must give to God the nerve center of his consent. He must surrender what to him is that which is most central, most frontal, most basic in his life, and that there will flow from this surrender not only right actions but

---

4. Howard Thurman, *Meditations of the Heart* (New York: Harper & Brothers, 1953), 104–5.

right relationships so that the kingdom of God moves within the life of the man and proceeds out of that center into the construct of his relations.

Jesus tells a story. We are calling it the great feast and in this designation there is no originality. He is illustrating another dimension of the kingdom of God. It is taken from a chapter in which there are several references to food and to being entertained at meals. But the great feast is something special. Here is a man who decides that he will have a grand banquet, and he invites all of the prestige-bearing people in his world. You know how we do. It's perfectly simple and very natural. We make out the list, and there are some people we like personally, but they won't quite fit into this, so we juggle the list, and finally we get our list made. This is what the man did. And he sent the invitations. And Jesus selects three refusals. There may have been many others in the story, but these are the three that have come down to us in the text. One of the men said, "I really ought to go. I would like to accept this invitation, but I have just bought some land, and it is very necessary for me to handle this affair. I must investigate it and so forth and so on. I'm sorry, but I can't accept." And the second one said, "I have just bought a pair of oxen, and I must test them." That's rather curious, that he would buy them before he tested them, but that's the story: He said, "I must test them. So I can't go, and you understand... business, before something else" [laughter]. And then the other man said, "I can't go, because I have just married." And that's all he said, he didn't ex... [laughter], he didn't explain anything. And then when the servant comes back to tell the man who was giving the banquet what had happened, he said, "The idea! Who do they think they are? Now you go out, and everybody who is broken down, lame, halt, blind, skinned and cast down like sheep without a shepherd, sick, unworthy, those who have long since withdrawn the citadel of themselves from any insistence upon a fundamental self-estimate, collect them all! Bring them."

And this was done. But there was still room. And this is very important... Once he shifted the grounds of his invitation and became inclusive, instead of being crowded, instead of having a feeling that he is being invaded as he became inclusive, he had more room. Interesting, but I won't push that. So he said, "Go beyond the city gates. Beat the bushes in other words, and bring everybody. My food will not taste right if there is any man within reach who is hungry."

Now that's the story. The kingdom of God is like that. Now there are many technical interpretations that may be given to the significance of this story against the background of Israel and the messianic hope. But I will not tarry with those. There are two or three other things that are crucial in it to which I would call your attention.

The first is very simple. That the persons who have every advantage are apt to be least mindful of the significance of their advantage and the responsibilities that flow from the advantage. Where I examine my own life, even as when you examine your life, is it not true that we tend always to relate ourselves to those in our world who are advantaged, who are prestige-bearing, who are in a position to give to us some measure of guarantee from association? How true it is. Who do you know? Who can say the right words?

There's a second thing. The man who is needy, the man who is without the normal guarantees by which the society places its imprimatur upon the personality, is apt to be far more reckless in his exposure of his wealth, his meagerness, his resources, his himself; he's apt to be more willing to run the risk, to stand up on behalf of someone whose need challenges him, because in simple language he has so little to lose, he has nothing to lose but his life, and he has long since learned how to wear his life like a loose garment. The kingdom of God seems to break through [to] him because the point at which in his life the pressures are greatest, it is at that point that the petition is thinnest between the movement of God and its bursting out. I hasten to add that this does not have to be true. It is apt to be true.

So, it is no accident that Jesus found some quality—you may guess it for yourselves—some peculiar quality among the publicans and the sinners. What do you think it was that he found? And he felt that somehow they were closer to all that God was trying to say to men than the good, the sure, the proud, the pompous, the controllers of the established order. And it makes one wonder if ever the keys to the kingdom can be in the hands of the powerful of the earth! Perhaps even the relentless movement of the spirit of the living God cannot quite immunize a man against the corruption of power. Maybe this is what he is talking about. The problem [is]: how can the kingdom of God come across the kingdoms of this world without becoming involved in all of the dynamics and the tragedies and the madness of power? I don't know the answer to this.

Now there's a third thing. We tend to be good, we tend to be moral, we tend to be religious and ethical as we move away from the areas of our security, while we tend to be immoral and unethical and irreligious as we move toward the citadel of our security. For instance, when you told a lie once, and I am not being personal altogether; when you told a lie once, and there wasn't anything at stake, you felt about it somewhat differently from the way you felt when you did not quite tell the truth when something very vital was at stake. When I am moving into the very heart of my profoundest preoccupation with the meaning of life and its significance in terms that I have accepted, when I am caught in the throb of my most meaningful involvements, I become ruthless, odd, insensitive, irresponsive, because I am afraid that if I open the door I must give up that which is to me more important than my life. So this wise one, this wonderfully tremendous personality, Jesus said, "Where your treasure is, where your preoccupation is, where your most profoundly moving involvement is, that's where you are, your heart, your pulse-beat, and this I must protect even against God." Until at last it turns ashes in my hand, and I am stripped to that which cannot be further reduced in me.

How difficult this is. I want to go to the feast. There are needs in me that cannot be satisfied unless I go to the feast. There are stirrings in me that cry out for fulfillment, but I am so busy. I have so many responsibilities; so much destiny turns on the decisions that I must make, moment after moment. This is what Darwin meant when he lamented the fact that once upon a time he loved music, his soul responded to poetry and beauty, but for so many years he had been weighing and measuring and giving his mind and thought over to the results of his scientific investigation that at sometime, he didn't know when, but this thing in him that had been fed by the music and by the beauty and by the poetry, this thing in him died. Sarah Teasdale talks about it, the woman who is climbing a hill, and she says, "When I get to the top how wonderful it will be! I can see many, many miles in many directions, and my lungs will be filled with pure, uncontaminated air. But the briars were always pulling in my gown, and every time I would look up, I would have to look down to disentangle myself." And at last she said, "I must have crossed the threshold some time ago, but the briars were always pulling in my gown, and now all the rest of the way will be only going down."

We see the dawn of this in the words of Jesus, "Man must not live by bread alone." I must expose the deepest hungers of me to the living God, even if it means cutting short some obligations, relaxing at some point some responsibility. It is I, the core of me that God wants, and when I expose that to him, everything else can be reduced to a manageable unit. This is his word. You are invited to the feast. What is your excuse?

PRAYER

Forgive us, O God, for the weakness of our minds and the faulty, faltering decrepitude of our words. Thou knowest the brooding that is deep within us. Accept as our sacrament the great depth of our desire. Walk beside us in the way that we take, and leave us not alone in our journey, our Father.

11

THE GREAT MOMENT

The Wedding Banquet
(Matthew 22:1-13)

In this sermon from his 1957 "Religion of Jesus" series,
Thurman tackles Matthew's more problematic version (the
wedding feast) of the parable found in in Luke 14:16-24 (the
great feast), which was discussed in the previous chapter.
Matthew turns Luke's parable of the social and economic
(religious) responsibility of the "haves" for the "have nots"
into an allegory of "salvation history" from an early Christian perspective: according to Matthew, the king represents
God; the ill-treated and killed servants represent the
prophets (cf. Matthew 5:11-12; 23:29-31, 37); those who mur-
dered the messengers represent the Jewish leaders who rejected the prophets; and the burning of the city symbolizes
the destruction of Jerusalem by the Romans in the 70 CE
war as punishment for the ill-treatment of the prophets by
the Jewish elite.

The second half of the parable, often thought to be a
later addition to the story, shifts the allegorical focus from
God's judgment on the Jewish elite who rejected the
prophets to those guests, bad and good alike, who are inside the wedding celebration. A man—either inexplicably
or understandably[1]—is without a wedding garment, the king/

---

1. Inexplicably, since this is a wedding feast; understandably,
since this man was not invited and was one of those "gathered" by the
servants, "bad and good alike." How was he supposed to be prepared

God reacts, the man cannot respond, and the king/God commands him to be "thrown into the outer darkness." The man's lack of seriousness (which probably symbolizes those followers who do not live up to their commitment and are morally unworthy to remain in the community)[2] inside the wedding celebration receives the ultimate punishment. Again, in this parable, as in several other parables, there is a separation of the worthy and unworthy—like the sheep and goats, the wheat and the chaff, and the wheat and the tares—at the final judgment.

Thurman reflects on the allegorical meaning of this second part of the parable: we are to respond to the radical demands of Jesus's message and, since there is "nothing that is outside of the Divine context," our response is the most important and fundamental response we make. Our response is, in fact, to the ultimate question, because it is our response to the purposes of God in our lives, to the God who is our creator and the creator of all things.

Thurman thus, as the parable implicitly does, connects this story of the man without a wedding garment to Jesus's saying, "For where your treasure is, there your heart will be also" (Matthew 6:21), a saying that Jesus illustrates with a number of parables (e.g., the treasure, Matthew 13:44; the pearl, Matthew 13:45-46). The proclamation of Jesus is indeed a challenge to respond that is addressed to everyone who has ears to hear, because Jesus speaks to the "ultimate question" to which all have to respond in one way or another, to the meaning of life itself. Every day on the journey that is our

---

with a wedding garment if he had not been given fair warning by an official invitation? It is possible, however, that all that is intended by "wedding garment" is a "clean garment." See Joachim Jeremias, *The Parables of Jesus* (New York: Charles Scribner's Sons, 1972), 187.

2. David Garland cites evidence that clothing can be used as "an apocalyptic image for moral unworthiness" (e.g., Revelation 3:4–5, 18; 6:11; 7:13–14; 22:14–15). See his *Reading Matthew* (New York: Crossroad, 1993), 221. Inclusion in the community means that you should be demonstrating the fruits of the Spirit (see chapter 9 in this book).

lives, on the paths we take and in the decisions we make, we are preparing ourselves, whether we realize it or not, for that great moment. And, as Thurman's example from Johan Boer's The Great Hunger *illustrates, when we respond to Jesus's commands, when we live out our lives as Jesus proclaims we should (such as by loving our enemies, Matthew 5:44), that is when the existence of God is evident in our lives and in our world.*

THE GREAT MOMENT

March 3, 1957

MEDITATION

We remember those experiences during the week that has passed in which we have been overwhelmed by a fresh manifestation of the grace and the care and the love of God. Our hearts voice their thanks to you and their praise. We are mindful of the ways by which we have felt sorry for things that we have done, and how we have wished that we could undo them and give to ourselves and those involved with us the fresh start and the new beginning. We remember those about whom and for whom we have cares and anxieties, those who are sick, and who find in the days that seem to stretch out before them no turning in the road. Those whose needs have somehow come through to us, and we would help, but we do not know how. We remember them, as we gather in our own spirits and our own minds before God. We turn without pretention and without self-praise, without pride to thee, our Father. Search our spirits, leave no stone unturned in our yards, that there may be nothing hidden from thee by our will or plan or our devices. It is so full of relief to us to be able to let down our

bars in thy presence, and to think and feel with freedom
and without inhibition, under thy scrutiny and surrounded
by thy love. Accept our lives as they are, our Father, and
grant that in this acceptance, we may be healed, strengthened, renewed, and redeemed, our Father.

SERMON

Continuing the teachings of the Master growing out of his
religious experience, I invite you to look at the story that he
tells that dramatizes the significance of the great moment
in a man's life. Very simple story. The banquet hall, the
king, or the one in whose honor the banquet is being held,
enters the door. At all the tables are those persons who
have responded to the invitation and are there to share in
the celebration of this great and significant moment. The
king with his retinue walks down the aisle between the tables. He is delighted with what he sees. Everybody is there
and has honored the occasion. Then he sees a man seated
at the table in his working clothes. Everybody else is
dressed for the occasion. He is there just as he came home.
We don't know what he did for a living. The king freezes in
his step. Points at him. Take him out. "Out into the darkness," Jesus suggests. That's all the story. A man who held
loosely and without meaning and significance a high moment. He came to the wedding feast with[out] the wedding
garment. He came to the banquet hall without the banquet
dress. He pretended that he was present and accounted for,
but he was absent. What does this mean?

It means many things to many people. In terms of the
religion of Jesus, what does this suggest? What does it say?
First of all, it suggests that in every person's life there is a
moment in which that life is exposed to confirmation, to
validation, to a radical demand. One does not ever quite
know when such a moment emerges. Sometimes it comes

at the very beginning of some undertaking. In the life and religious experience of Jesus, it came at the time of his baptism, when at last he was able to bring himself to a point of full and complete and deliberate self-conscious devotion to what to him was the highest end, the most significant meaning of life, and when, with all his passionate endeavor, he responded to this, the heavens opened. It seemed that the living spirit of the living God lighted upon his shoulder in the form of a dove, and deep within himself, he heard the voice of God say, "This is right. I am pleased. Well pleased." It matters little, you see, about the ways subsequent to this experience by which life seems to say that the experience had no meaning, the experience was not what you thought it was.

You remember in "Paracelsus," Browning suggests that Paracelsus was a wanderer looking for this moment when the heavens would open and he would see on the horizon of his dreams and his aspirations the city which was that toward which his whole life moved. Then it happened. The clouds opened, and he saw the city, and the clouds came back together. Paracelsus says, I can find my way now because I have seen the city, and that view no darkness can obscure. This puts it in a very dramatic dimension. But for most of us, life does not move that way. For most of us we live and function along lines that are ordinary and commonplace, and we may say that for us there is no great moment.

Let us take another look. I want you to reach back in your thinking to the basic insistence of Jesus about God and how God relates to life, for it is in that context that the next observation belongs.

God is the creator of life. God is the creator of existence. God is the creator of the living substance. There is nothing that is outside of the divine context. The totality of a man's life as well as the totality of existence is within the frame of reference of the Divine, of God, to be very specific about it. This suggests, then, that the purpose of life, the ends of life, the goals of life, even the fundamental direction of life, all of this is more important and more crucial than my little purposes, and my little hopes, and my little dreams. Every aspiration that I have, however simple and commonplace that may be, every upward thrust of my mind and my spirit toward even little ends is bottomed by the movement of the purposes of God in life. Whenever with my little purpose I am able to see my little purpose in a larger context and in a larger meaning, this lifts my little purpose and my little meaning into a dimension that transcends my little purpose and my little meaning. Sometimes it happens in the most traumatic ways.

Here is a man who is sick. He gets a good doctor. The doctor practices medicine with reference to him. [The man] gets well. Now, such a man may deal with his illness at the level of ordinary natural processes. There is a rational understanding for the disease, and a specific [remedy] developed in the light of that, and he is healed and goes on his way. But he may deal with his illness in another dimension. At the time of his illness he may think about the total meaning of his life. He may use this experience as a time when he reappraises all of his life, all of the things to which he is devoting his energies. He may rethink himself and experience the livingness of his life and see what it is that he is after, what is the direction in which he is going, where is his treasure, what are the ends which he is seeking, what does life mean to him. His illness becomes a windbreak behind which he tarries to get a sense of total bearing. He discovers that perhaps for the first time he is raising about his life an ultimate question, and the moment he begins to raise the ultimate question about the meaning of his life, he becomes involved in meanings and ends that transcend his little life, and he works now to align his life in terms of these so that the strength of living, the strength of the meaning of existence would be for him a resource upon which he draws in order to give to his commonplace experience now the timeless significance, and a new dignity, and a new strength.

There is a third thing to say. The living of a man's life, day by day, is the only preparation for the great moment. Day by day. If I may illustrate this without seeming to be talking out of turn, we see it demonstrated in classwork. The only preparation for examinations is day by day. The great moment is never something that is irrelevant to the life you are living, to the way you are taking, to the journey you are making. I won't say any more about this.

Sometimes it is with reference to doing that which we resist doing because of experiences of injury or because of experiences of hostility, but when I am able to bring myself to the place that I can forgive somebody who wronged me, when I can be kind to someone with whom the logic of the situation quite naturally would demand unkindness, when I am able to do this, then a very extraordinary thing happens, the heavens do open, and I get a confirmation of my roots, so that it is really for my own health and my own self that incidentally I forgive the injury. When the hero of "The Great Hunger" decided that he could not bring himself to the point that his life could be settled for returning an injury in kind when his neighbor's dog killed his girl, when he found that even though he wasn't a good man, he wasn't trying to be a saint, he was just an ordinary man who loved his family, and who loved his child, but somehow he could not accept the general and unanimous judgment of the environment that the man who owned the dog should not be given any grain with which to plant his fields so that when the long winter night came, he and his wife would slowly starve to death as compensation for the violence of this beast, he got up out of his bed and dressed, went down into his cellar, took his basket, filled it with grain, and under the cover of darkness, climbed this man's fence, made the furrows, sowed his enemy's field with grain, not

because God told him to do it, not because he was responding to some great external moral judgment being passed
upon his life, but deep within himself, he felt now a great
responsibility, and he had to plant his enemy's field with
grain that God might exist, and when he did it, for the first
time in his life, he felt that an act of his had now related to
him all the meaning that there is in the universe, and he
could never again be as one who lived without resources.

Do not shrink, then, from that which turns up in your
road, suddenly making of you an ultimate demand. Know
that if you respond with all that you have, your little life
takes on a meaning in the light of which even death itself is
a little thing. To miss it because of fear, timidity, pride, arrogance, self-righteousness, deceit, to miss it is to wander
down your road in darkness, and what a darkness, what a
darkness it is for you.

Go thy way, all things say. Thou hast thy way to go. Thou
hast thy time to live. Do thy thing. Know thou this, that
there is no other who can do for thee that which is appointed thee of God. So go thy way and do thy thing.

BENEDICTION

Dismiss us with thy Spirit, O God, and let us not wander in
the darkness, in the darkness.

12

MOOD TO LINGER

The Prodigal Son
(Luke 15:11–32)

"Don't ask yourself what the world needs. Ask your-self what makes you come alive, and go do that, be-cause what the world needs is people who have come alive..."[1]

Thurman's brief reflection in this chapter illustrates one of the foundational elements of his spirituality: we should cultivate the mood to linger. The world and our lives are filled with distractions, and it is critical to seek the quiet; to spend time in solitude, reflection, and meditation; to use this time to reflect deeply on life's ultimate questions and our own direction.

Thurman's guidance for our spirituality is reminiscent of Buddhism's call for mindfulness: the "energy" to experi-ence deeply everything that happens in the present moment —note Thurman's advice to linger over the richness of food, such as bread that is "thoughtfully and carefully prepared." To live in the moment.

Thurman's counsel, then, is similar that of the Bud-dhist monk, Thich Nhat Hanh, who uses the parable of

---

1. Howard Thurman in a private conversation with Gil Bailie as described in: Gil Bailie, *Violence Unveiled: Humanity at the Cross-roads* (New York: Crossroad, 1995), xv.

the mustard seed to speak about God being within our consciousness:

> What is the seed? Where is the soil? What is it if not
> our own consciousness? We hear repeatedly that God
> is within us. To me, it means that God is within our
> consciousness. Buddha nature, the seed of mindful-
> ness, is in the soil of our consciousness. It may be
> small, but if we know how to care for it, how to
> touch it, how to water it moment after moment, it
> becomes an important refuge for all the birds of the
> air. It has the power of transforming everything.[2]

For Nhat Hanh, like Thurman, the growth of the "seed"
occurs because we are "mindful"; we take the time for conscious action and practice, and the world can be changed on
the foundation of our own transformation:

> The practices of prayer and meditation help us
> touch the most valuable seeds that are within us,
> and they put us in contact with the ground of our
> being…When the energy of mindfulness is present,
> transformation takes place. When the energy of the
> Holy Spirit is within you, understanding, love,
> peace, and stability are possible. God is within.[3]

To that extent, Thurman would agree. Perhaps that is
why he included a sermon on the Buddha in his 1953 "Men
Who've Walked with God" series.[4] But Thurman in this sermon chooses another mystic, Meister Eckhart, to illustrate
what he means "to live out of your center" (Eckhart's the
"uncreated element").

---

2. Thich Nhat Hanh, *Living Buddha, Living Christ* (New York:
Riverhead Books, 1995), 155. For an analysis, see David B. Gowler, *The
Parables after Jesus* (Grand Rapids, MI: Baker Academic, 2017), 249–53.

3. Nhat Hanh, *Living Buddha, Living Christ*, 167–68.

4. https://bit.ly/2EnWc3E.

To live out of your inmost center, your core, requires cultivation. This cultivation requires time, quietness, and meditation, and it is through the practice of cultivation that we have our primary and most basic encounter with God, as Thurman's brilliant example illustrates: It was only in the post-midnight silence that Thurman could hear the flow of the water in the Erie Canal under Main Street in Rochester, New York.

Instead of the parable of the mustard seed, Thurman returns again to the parable of the prodigal son to explain what happens when we take the time for quiet meditation: we are able to "come to ourselves," and, when we do that, we ultimately come to God our Father. As Thurman says, "That which is deepest in me is always reaching out to that which is deepest in life," and that is how we reach "wholeness."

What was true in 1958 about the hustle and bustle of our daily lives is even more true today. But even in the midst of the daily chaos of our lives—indeed, because of it— we can afford to take a few minutes of quiet and solitude to listen to Thurman's words and, perhaps, follow his sage counsel.

MOOD TO LINGER

April 18, 1958

OPENING PRAYER

Let the words of my mouth and the meditation of my heart be acceptable in thy sight, O Lord, my strength and my redeemer.

READING

As a background this morning, I am reading from my book,
Deep is the Hunger.[5]

> It does not require the expert knowledge of the psy-
> chologist to discover that we live daily under condi-
> tions that undermine whatever tendencies there are
> in the human spirit that make for a relaxed way of
> life. Everyone is in a hurry. There is little time left
> for the deep experiencing of the facets of life that
> make up the daily round. In our homes, someone
> spends many hours in planning, shopping for, and
> preparing food. Mealtime often is something to be
> rushed through in the shortest possible time. Thou-
> sands of years were spent in the developing of our
> taste buds. We scarcely use them now. What a joy it
> is to linger over the taste of food! In a simple thing
> like bread that is thoughtfully and carefully pre-
> pared, one may taste the richness of wheat or corn
> or barley that in its growth absorbed sunlight and
> rain and the rich chemistry of the soil. All the ingre-
> dients besides should serve to reveal and make avail-
> able what the grain has stored up in its life under
> the skies. Or take the matter of conversation. Go
> back over the days of this very week. How much
> good talk have you had? What a history a word re-
> veals of the strivings and triumphs of the human
> spirit! Do we select our words with the kind of rever-
> ence that bespeaks a recognition of the treasure

---

5. *Howard Thurman, Deep is the Hunger* (New York: Harper &
Brothers, 1951), 153–54. The reading on this recording is slightly mod-
ified from the published text.

house they bear? The spoken word is the symbol of meanings that we try to convey by conversation. Our conversation is hurried, feverish, hectic. Our spirits do not have time to use our words as lungs through which they breathe. To have a good talk, to have times of sharing through the spoken word deep things of the mind and spirit, leisure to search for the right word that is capable of channeling the stirring of things within—this is to have the mood to linger in conversation. Or take the matter of a sense of direction for your own life. Do you ever take time to ask, "What is my point? What am I trying to do with my own life?" All travelers somewhere along the way find it necessary to check their course, to see how they are doing. We wait until we are sick or shocked into stillness before we do the commonplace thing of getting our bearings. And yet we wonder why we are depressed, why we are unhappy, why we lose our friends, why we are ill-tempered. This condition we pass on to our children, our husbands, our wives, our associates, our friends. Cultivate the mood to linger. If you do not know how to start, or if the conditions under which you live make it difficult, try getting up earlier in the morning and establishing a meditation period. Who knows? God may whisper to you in the quietness what he has been trying to say to you for so a long time through the noise and the bustle of your life.

REFLECTION

Do you live out of your surface self, or do you live out of your center? It seems to me that we live again and again out of the surface self, the more superficial aspect of our lives without referring to the innermost center, to that dimension of life that represents the nerve center of our consent.

It is my deep conviction that at the core—not only of life in general—but at the core of human life, at the inmost center of human life, there is what Meister Eckhart long ago called, the "uncreated element," an element that is not exclusively of the self, but an element which, in my language, is God. And when we move out of this deepest center, when we relate to life out of the deepest things in our life, then the response which we get is from the deepest thing in life. So, that which is deepest in me reaches out to that which is deepest in life, and if I can come to this dimension in my living, then I seem to myself to be a whole and integrated and unified person.

Now this requires quiet. It requires the cultivation not only of a certain kind of leisure, but, more importantly, the cultivation of what may be called a sense of leisure. It means centering down, it means quieting of all of the inner noises that are going on in life with reference to which we react in ways of tension and anxiety.

Now, it is at this level, it seems to me, that man has his primary and most basic encounter with God. And so many things of which we are not aware when we are living at a more superficial level, we become aware of in the stillness, when all the noises, the interior noises, are quieted.

I remember many years ago walking down Main Street in Rochester, New York. It was after midnight, and there was no traffic on the street, streetcars had disappeared, and [there was] only an occasional automobile. I could hear my footfall as I walked along the sidewalk. And, then, I heard another thing. Something which seemed to be the flowing of water, and it followed me all the length of the street until I turned off. The next day I was talking with one of my professors about this, a man who had grown up in Rochester. And he said, "You did hear water. You were not deluded, because underneath Main Street, there is a part of the Erie Canal. And when the traffic is going on in the middle of the day and during the early evening, this noise crowds out the murmur of this flowing water underneath the Main Street."

So much of our lives is that way. There are things of which you cannot become aware, things you cannot sense until at last all of the surface confusion and chaos and noise of your life is somehow quieted. And it is then that your ears pick up sounds that come from the deeper regions of your life.

It is recorded in the New Testament in the story of the prodigal son that when he was able to "come to himself," it was then that he came to his father. That which is deepest in me is always reaching out to that which is deepest in life. And when these two come together then I have a sense of being whole, and this can only be done when in many, many ways and in many aspects of our lives, we cultivate quiet, we study ways by which we can reduce the traffic of our days.

One day one of my students wrote a very interesting appendix to a paper which he had prepared for me in a course. It seemed that during the war, he had been a deep sea diver. As a matter of fact, he was a deep sea diver by profession. After the war he decided that he would become an artist and was studying art in many of its aspects. He told in this appendix about an experience which he had at the bottom of the Caribbean Sea. He said that he had maybe two hours at his disposal, and he was sent down—I don't remember how many fathoms now—to look around and to investigate certain things. He decided, since he was in no hurry, that he would sit on one of the large coral rocks and observe the life around him. So he sat, and he described how various fishes came up and looked at him through his glasses, and he would wink his eye at them and play little quiet jokes. And then suddenly he realized that he was sitting in the midst of what seemed to him to be a flower garden. He admired the forms, the shapes, and even the colors as they were reflected from the sun that came from the surface of the water. And then he realized that time was passing, and he needed to be about his business. And he began moving, and as soon as he moved, every flower in this garden disappeared. It seemed that these were plant animals [in] that mid-passage dimension of life, and when he became still and became a part of the landscape, then in that quietness, all of the beautiful colors and the beautiful shapes of this form of life around him blossomed. What he could not see and experience when he was moving around became clear and possible to him when he became quiet enough to blend himself with the fabric, with the very substance, of the life around him.

And this seems to me to be characteristic of life, and from this we may get a very simple parable: that when we learn how to be quiet, when we learn how to center down and to get rid of the surface noises, it is then [that], at the deepest thing in us, there begins a movement which not only is creative but is redemptive for all our days.

BENEDICTION

Let the words of my mouth and the meditation of my heart be acceptable in thy sight, O Lord, my strength and my redeemer.

13

WHO IS MY NEIGHBOR?

The Good Samaritan
(Luke 10:25–37)

The parable of the prodigal son and the parable of the Good Samaritan are central to Thurman's religious thought and experience. For that reason, we include another example— out of many others—of Thurman's reflections on the parable of the good Samaritan. This example comes from a sermon Thurman delivered on November 25, 1956, five years after the sermon on the Good Samaritan in chapter 5 of this volume. The sermon that follows is the third in the "Religion of Jesus" series, which Thurman delivered at Boston University's Marsh Chapel.

One of the major implications of the "God centered" religious experience of Jesus, Thurman argues, is that Jesus expects God "to invade the normal processes of life." God is present in all things, in both the mundane and the extraordinary, and we are called to "work with" God to further God's kingdom, a kingdom that is present among us, within us, and in our "community relatedness."

Thurman's sermon challenges assumptions of community relatedness, including family relationships. He notes that Jesus proclaimed that one's true family was whoever does God's will (e.g., Mark 3:35). A true family is an intentional relationship created by those who unite in a working relationship, with God and other human beings, to bring about God's kingdom, "to be to each other not only what God would have them to be, but what God is to each other."

This sermon, then, like the majority of Thurman's interpretations of the Good Samaritan parable, focuses on our responsibilities to other human beings because of our status as children of God who are of infinite worth. *Our own personal transformation leads to societal transformation through the building of human relations and true community once we correctly answer the question, "Who is my neighbor?"*

Thurman's story about one of his student's retelling of the Good Samaritan parable serves as a modern version of the way Jesus's parable would have jolted its hearers: by portraying religious people "respected" in their day as examples of how not to behave and by providing a surprising example of someone who acts in the way we are supposed to act.[1]

Thurman opens our eyes, as Jesus did before him, to the ways in which we limit and constrain our "neighbors," our community, and our "family." We are to treat other human beings as the Good Samaritan treated the man by the side of the road not because we are related to them by race, creed, nationality, or any other human-created community; we are to break all such artificial boundaries and treat others as God treats us, because all of us are children of God and because we become involved in a deliberate encounter from the core of ourselves to the core of other human beings. It is then and only then that we become followers of the religion of Jesus: "Anything less than this is unworthy of our creation as children of God."

---

1. Compare the story in this sermon with the longer version in Howard Thurman, *With Head and Heart: The Autobiography of Howard Thurman* (New York: Harcourt Brace Jovanovich, 1979), 176–77.

WHO IS MY NEIGHBOR?

November 25, 1956

MEDITATION

It is good to remember that God has not left himself without a witness in our spirits, that despite all of the wanderings of our footsteps, despite all of the ways by which we have sought to circumvent his truth within us, despite all of the weaknesses of spirit and of mind and resoluteness of body, despite all of the blunders by which we have isolated ourselves from our fellows and proven unworthy of the love and the trust and the confidence by which again and again our faltering lives are surrounded, despite all of this, it is good to remember in the quietness that God has not left himself without a witness in our lives.

We turn, therefore, to thee, our Father; lay bare our secret waiting for the penetration of thy light upon us, that we may be healed and forgiven and confirmed anew to the end, our Father, that we may walk in thy way and live in thy light. We thank thee; we thank thee, our Father, that thou hast not left us alone to the devices of our minds and our spirits, but within us and about us there is thy witness, and for this, for this, our Father, we rejoice to give to thee the thanks of our hearts this day.

SERMON

We begin our thinking about the religion of Jesus by calling to mind with great repetition, and perhaps wearying insistence, that the religion of Jesus was God centered. In the second instance, according to the religion of Jesus man must not be deluded into acceptance of the apparent dualism and contradiction in experience. He who expects God to invade the normal processes of life, to upset the relentless logic of antecedent and consequences, as manifest in the moral law and natural law, [would be] in the mind and the thought and the religious experience of Jesus acting as one who did not believe that God is the creator of life, that God is a worker in human history, and we are called upon to work with him. "I ask no dream, no prophet ecstasies, no sudden rending of the veil of clay, but take the dimness of my soul away." Always close at hand and the living stuff of the living process of the living world of the living universe is the living God. That was his religion. Today we take it a step further.

Who is my neighbor? The old man in the Book of Luke who has come to the end of his days bursts into song about Jesus: "This child is the sign of man's attack." The working arrangement under which life is lived as a part of the customary pattern of behavior among mankind, this was under attack by the religion of Jesus. For we operate on the assumption and the theory that community relatedness is basically rooted in an organic structure of some kind. The organic structure of blood, for instance. This is my family, and by blood, by the intimate unfolding of the organic process that resulted particularly in my being born into this world, this is, after all, the very essence, the very cement of community.

Now, that is the way we operated then, and now Jesus said with reference to this, "Who is my mother? Who is my father? Who is my sister or my brother? He who does the will of God." The organic relationship is not the binding relationship for community. We operate on the theory and the assumption [of] the race structure: this man belongs to my kind; "I am a son of Abraham," said the Pharisee to Jesus, and as a son of Abraham this is the binding tie (Jesus made use of this in another connection with apparent contradiction!—[see Luke 13:10–17]). It is this that marks me off from my fellows and places them there and places me here. Against that gulf, across that gulf, no man comes unless he too is a son of Abraham. You are a son of Abraham not because you are a Jew, said Jesus. You are a son of Abraham only if you do the work of Abraham. The community cannot rest upon that kind of organic structure. We assume that the working relationship is built upon something we call nationality. There were many lepers, said Jesus, in Israel, but only Namaan, the Syrian, was healed by the prophet.

What does all this mean? What is his religion hammering at? It is this: that community is rooted in the quality of deliberate intention. It is the lifting into focus into the mind of the intent to express in the structure of relations the purpose of God in the creation of man. And what is the purpose of God in the creation of man? Here, on the earth, not in the heavens, not at the end of life, when the spirit takes wings somewhere, but here on the earth, the purpose of God in the creation of man is the establishing of his kingdom of persons, united in the intent to be to each other not only what God would have them to be, but what God is to each other.

This is revolutionary, and it is very, very difficult. It is disturbing to the mind and to the conscience. For it says [that] what I must do is make as part of the center of my hard core of purpose in the living of my life from day to day what is constitutional in me by virtue of the fact that I am a child of God. That what is a part of the untutored movement of the life of God in me must move up to the center of my awareness and become for me a part of the deliberate intention of my life. Where this does not happen, there is no community. You have seen it, haven't you? Here is a mother and a father and children in a family unit, but because they are tied together in this way, there may not be community between them. Under what circumstances does community enter into their organic relationship? When the members of this primary social unit begin to put at the center of their behavior toward each other a deliberate intent to love, to trust, to be kind, to be gracious, to recognize no boundaries to community.

That's what Jesus is talking about. They may be related to each other in these organic ways but there is no community until this happens. Now, when there does arise in a man this deliberate intention, a curious thing takes place, for now he has that which more and more structures his daily behavior, his thinking, all the details of his life. There is erected in him a principle of integration around which his life more and more moves, and all of the materials of his life, including the materials of his personality, become the agent of this deliberate intent.

Now, who is my neighbor? A man went from Jerusalem to Jericho, and he fell among thieves. I cannot ever read that parable without remembering an experience I had the first year I came to the university. I tell it with some—I did not intend to tell it, but I've got to now because it keeps shuttling in and out of my mind, and in order to get rid of it, I'll tell you. It was a class that I had once a week of men who were just entering the school, and they were taking a course in homiletics, and I had them for this one hour. One of the men chose to take this story and make it the center of his fifteen-minute meditation. He read the story very quietly; then he closed the book, and he said, "Now I want to tell you what Jesus meant":

A man was walking from Boston University Field down to Kenmore Square. It was about dusk. He came alongside the School of Theology, and there was a man hiding in the bush who jumped him, and did what his violence made possible, and left the man just inside the little wire fence to fend for himself. Then, the Dean of the Chapel came walking by, but he was very anxious to get to Robinson Chapel to have a meditation period, and he didn't see the man, or if he saw him he looked through him into the Robinson Chapel. And then the next person to come by, well, I will let that person be nameless, but he is also somebody you would recognize, and he passed. And then a custodian came by and saw the man in this condition, and the first thing that he did after getting close to the man and realizing that he was a cigarette smoker, he lighted a cigarette and gave it to the man and that comforted him. And then he took him into the School of Theology, and all the rest of it follows.

[The student] didn't mean any harm by what he was saying, but he was pointing up the fact that the boundaries of community are set, not by the circumstance, not by the position, not by the equipment... the boundaries of community are set by the deliberate intent of the heart and the mind, and if the deliberate intent of the heart and the mind are of the same quality and essence as is the deliberate intent of God in the creation of man that there may be on this earth a community of friendly men under a friendly sky, then this commitment dominates the little deed and the big deed, the little grace and the greatest sacrifice, the little tenderness and the great act of redemption. If I am unable to do this, if I do not work at this, even though I may say my prayers, bow my knees before the altar, profess the regeneration of the heart in the redemption of my life, I am not a follower of the religion of Jesus. [The religion of

Jesus means] to make as the deliberate intention of my life to be to you what the purpose of God demands that I be to you, that in so doing, I enter into his kingdom, and he enters into my life. Anything less than this is unworthy of our creation as children of God. Jesus stands at the door of our sanctuary watching the struggling, struggling multitudes move down the broad highway of the age, weeping, weeping, for they do not know what they do.

PRAYER

Forgive us, our Father, for our failure. Inspire our hearts to find within us the way, that we may enter into thy kingdom and thy kingdom may enter into us. Dismiss us with thy spirit, O God, and grant unto us thy peace.

14

JUSTICE AND MERCY

The Unmerciful Servant
(Matthew 18:1–35)

Justice, mercy, reconciliation, forgiveness, and restoration of community are almost ubiquitous themes in Thurman's sermons on the parables, and perhaps that is why he concentrates so much on the parables that demonstrate those themes, such as the parables of the lost coin, lost sheep, and lost son, as well as his sermons in this volume that discuss the two debtors and the unmerciful servant (see chapter 4).

This sermon, "Justice and Mercy," could just as easily be entitled, "Reconciliation and Forgiveness." Justice, as Thurman notes, is the restoration of balance or, in the words of Lester Ward, "the artificial equalization of unequals." An underlying and not explicitly stated rationale behind Thurman's arguments in this sermon is, as we have seen again and again in these sermons, his underlying belief in the formation and sustaining of community. God is not the equal of human beings, but God acts with justice—thus artificially equalizing unequals—and mercy, forgiving human beings and therefore showing the way for human beings to reconcile with each other. As Thurman's use of the parable of the unmerciful servant indicates, those human beings who have been forgiven by God (cf. the man who forgives the man who owed him "two million dollars"; chapter 4) should treat their fellow human beings in the grace-filled way God has treated them, with justice (with "voluntary distance"), forgiveness, love, compassion, and mercy. Reconciliation, the restoration of community, is the result. In the parable, a lack of such mercy results in God's judgment upon those who, having received God's mercy, themselves act without mercy. A better translation of Matthew 18:33, in fact, is: "Is it not necessary for you to have had mercy on your fellow servant, as I had on you!" God's grace and mercy bring responsibilities for those receiving them, including a responsibility to restore human community though such merciful reconciliation.

The federal judge in South Carolina to whom Thurman in this sermon refers is J. Waties Waring. In the 1940s, Waring issued a number of rulings that challenged Jim Crow laws, including one that eventually helped lead to the Supreme Court's Brown v. Board of Education decision. Judge Waring not only integrated his court staff, but his legal decisions included ordering equal pay for African-American school teachers in South Carolina and, as Thurman notes in his sermon, allowing African Americans to vote in primaries. Most famously, the 1951 Briggs v. Elliott case involved Waring urging the NAACP lawyer Thurgood Marshall to challenge the "separate but equal" Plessy v. Ferguson decision directly and end the legal foundation for segregation in public schools. The case was lost 2-1 (and appealed), but Waring's argument in his dissent—that "segregation is per se inequality"—was cited in the Supreme Court's Brown v. Board of Education 9-0 ruling. Because of his courageous stands, Waring became a pariah in his hometown of Charleston and later moved to New York.[1]

There are numerous insights in this sermon that deserve exploration, such as the integrity of the moral order, but we will take Thurman's lead and say that we "need

---

1. See the April 10, 2014 (4:44 pm) episode of "Code Switch: Race and Identity, Remixed": *How the Son of a Confederate Soldier became a Civil Rights Hero*: https://www.npr.org/sections/codeswitch/2014/04/10/301432659/how-the-son-of-a-confederate-soldier-became-a-civil-rights-hero.

not illustrate that." What is especially intriguing, however, are Thurman's insights into the use and abuse of power. Is there ever such a thing, Thurman wonders, as "legitimate power?" Thurman also offers deep insights into the differences between justice and mercy, the "voluntary distance" that Jesus and the Psalmist promote, and the fact that when human beings impose power over other human beings, when they impose their will upon others, they reduce those other human beings into mere objects. True community can never occur under those circumstances. Jesus's parable of mercy and forgiveness of such a large debt brilliantly illustrates, though the use of a negative example of ingratitude and the resulting abuse of power by the first servant upon the second, that God's mercy to us should be replicated in our own lives, that we should be grateful not just to God but also to the principle of mercy, and that we should show such mercy to others. God's mercy should be creative and redemptive, and when we love others as God has loved us, when we forgive others as God has forgiven us, when we show mercy to others as God has shown mercy to us, that lifts us "into the category of an authentic child of God" and restores our community with God and with other human beings.

JUSTICE AND MERCY

January 22, 1956

MEDITATION

The great silence that surrounds us as we together share the spirit and the love of God throws us back upon ourselves: deepening our insights into the meaning of our lives, revealing to us in the quietness the lights and the shadows of our days, defining for us the significance of our deeds during the past week, the doors of truth and understanding, in the presence of which we stood on Monday, Tuesday, Wednesday, Thursday, Friday, or Saturday and refused to enter; the consequences of the hurried word uttered in a moment of irritation or anxiety, a word which we could not recall, but as we watched with bated breath its fearful consequences unfolding before our eyes in the life of another, in the quietness we portrayed before us the meaning of some of the larger events by which our common life is surrounded, events having to do with the fates of nations and peoples, events having to do with the future peace and health of the world—all of these things move before our view as we sit in the midst of the congregation but each in his own isolation enveloped by the stillness, the quiet, the presence of God. We ask no dream, no prophetic ecstasy, no sudden rending of the veil of clay, but take the dimness of our souls away, while there is still time, and for us, O God, our Father, this is enough, this is enough for us.[2]

SERMON

If I were to use a text for my reflections this morning, many come to mind. "He hath not dealt with us after our sins nor rewarded us according to our iniquity" [Psalm 103:10]. Or another, "Be not deceived. God is not mocked. Whatsoever a man soweth, that shall he also reap" [Galatians 6:7]. Or another, "Vengeance is mine. I will repay, saith the Lord" [Deuteronomy 32:35; Romans 12:19]. Or another, "Blessed are the merciful, for they shall obtain mercy" [Matthew 5:7].

---

2. Thurman then reads from the Egyptian Book of the Dead and Olive Schreiner, "The Sunlight Lay across My Bed."

One of my young undergraduate friends, when the topic was set, said that it showed rather bad taste to have a topic like this during final examinations.

Justice, according to America's first and pioneer sociologist, Lester Ward, was defined as the artificial equalization of unequals, the restoration of balance, or equilibrium, in a situation in which the particular balance, or the particular equilibrium, has been upset. It raises no question about the fundamental character of the status quo that is reestablished. We see a figure of justice that has come down to us from another period—the blindfolded woman with the scales in her hand, the blindfold is there because the idea is that justice should not be influenced by any considerations that may be available to the person if he were swayed by his emotions. When Judge—can't think of his name at the moment, but it doesn't matter—a federal judge of a certain district in South Carolina, some years ago, not many years ago, was called upon to make a ruling about the legal rights of suffrage as these rights were being interpreted by the Democratic primary in the state of South Carolina, he arrived at a decision on the basis of his interpretation, as he put it, of the application of the Jeffersonian doctrine of democracy to the statute. He had no interest in consequences one way or another. He detached himself from his background of life and thought and training and conditioning in the state of South Carolina and interpreted the law only to discover that when he did interpret the law in the light of the meaning of the law as he saw it, detached from his emotional conditioning or his intellectual conditioning, he found himself in the midst of great emotional turmoil, and the consequences were so devastating that finally he established residence in another part of the United States.

Justice, to mention the word, sends our minds hurtling over a wide variety of things which do not of essence concern us for our consideration, for I want us to think about the meaning of justice and mercy in terms of our innermost sense, not only of rightness, but our innermost sense of the significance of life and existence and the meaning of God.

I have two basic considerations to explore. One is that men appeal to justice when they are dealing with each other from within a context of equality of wills, and neither has the power to inflict his will upon the other. In the stalemate, justice is appealed to as that which is outside of the context. Now I need not illustrate that.

There is another sense in which men appeal to justice, and this is in line with my thinking this morning. When we are in a situation in which we have power, legitimate power, if there is ever such a thing, over another human being, and we relax that power and establish within ourselves voluntary distance between the expression of our power and ourselves—now let's talk about that: when we are in a position of power over another human being, and we do not exercise that power, but we voluntarily establish distance within ourselves between the full-orbed operation and expression of our power and ourselves. You do it with your children, don't you? Every parent has power over the will of his child up to a certain point. I remember once having to deal with this—many times, but one incident occurs to me now—when I was reading something, and I had to finish reading it before going on to do something else that took me out of the house, and one of our daughters who was very young, about three and a half, came rushing in, and she said, "Daddy, there's something that I want you to do for me and with me now." And I said, "But I can't do that now. You see, I'm reading this book, and I've got to finish it before a certain time," and that made no impression. But she insisted. Then I repeated what I [had] said but, for a moment, I closed the book and put a rumble in my voice that surrounded her with a certain atmosphere of insecurity, and then she bristled and stood her ground and finally in disgust she went out of the room with her will untouched by mine. Now I was not willing to establish voluntary distance, but I stood on my parental constitutional grounds.

Now let's think about that now. Jesus talks about it. Do you remember? "Ye have been told that an eye for an eye, a tooth for a tooth," and that was some advance for [an] earlier justice, that [said] if a man injures me then there is only [one] limitation that I should recognize in inflicting injury upon him and that is my strength or perhaps his endurance. Then, there is a step further. Justice meant if a man put my eye out, then I had the right to put his eye out. The measure of what I inflicted upon him was determined beforehand by the measure of what he had inflicted upon me. [However], Jesus says, "There is something else here. When a man inflicts an injury upon me, I must establish voluntary distance with him, between what I would do to him, and what I do to him." Now this is what the Psalmist and what the men of religious insight insist upon as the basis of the relationship between God and man...The will of God...introduces into his relationship with men this voluntary distance between what he is able to do—or between what seems to be the immediate result of the deed that the individual performs—and what he wills to do in the situation. "He hath not dealt with us after our sins, nor rewarded us according to our iniquities" [Psalm 103:10 (KJV)].

Now let's see what this means now in terms of mercy. See where we are. Justice is appealed to in a situation of radical equality in which there is a power stalemate, and justice then becomes a kind of referee that determines the deed on considerations that have nothing to do with power; extenuating circumstances may enter in. Justice is appealed to when individuals are in situations that are unequal in terms of the power which they are able to exercise,

and the person who is in a position of power relaxes the
logic of his power in its fulfillment and voluntarily estab-
lishes within himself and his procedures, his attitude, [and]
his will voluntary distance between the fulfillment of his
power over the other person and what he actually does.
Now, when a man exercises power over another in the
sense of the imposition of his will upon another, a very curious thing happens. It reduces the other person to a thing.
When I exercise my will, and I strip the other person of the
precious ingredient of his personality that gives to him a
private autonomous existence . . . I render him as a thing in
my hands. Now when I relax my power, and establish voluntary distance within myself in this regard, then I permit his
integrity of will, of mind, of personality, to remain intact
without regard to my control over him, or what may be regarded by me as his just desserts for his infraction of my
will . . . The merciful act, then, is the act in which an individual engages when he is willing to refrain from the exercise
of the logic of his power over another and introduces into
the relationship a principle that transcends the power relationship between him and another. Now mercy, then, is
what a person experiences when he is aware of the fact that
he could have been victimized by a power over him, but was
not. And his response [to] being spared from this is in
terms of gratitude, but not gratitude in terms of to the person who spared him but gratitude to this principle, this
quality, in human life that enables one man to withhold the
fulfillment of his will because of considerations that transcend the necessity to fulfill his will.

You remember how Jesus dealt with this in another
parable. Here was a man who owed another man a lot of
money, and he went to the man to whom he owed the
money, and he said, "Times are pretty difficult, and I wish
you would do something about this. You can throw me into
jail but be kind to me." And he settled it in a way that was

creative and redemptive, relieved him of certain aspects of
the obligation, and he went away rejoicing. Then as he was
walking down the street full of the elixir of this wonderful
feeling, he saw a man that owed him, and he said, "I want
to see you." And when he saw him, he said, "What about it?"
And the man said, "Times are difficult, you know that."
[And the man replied], "That has nothing to do with it.
You are under obligation to pay me, the time is up, and I
want my money or you take the consequences."

Now Jesus says that that's the way one man who was
grateful—the first man was grateful to the other man for
excusing him—... did not have the added grace which was
the recognition of what was at work in the other man that
enabled the other man to deal with him in this way. If he
had had insight into that, then that would have been his
clue to [seek] within himself the quality that he had seen in
its glory in the other man who had blessed his life, and he
would have applied it to this man.

Now what does all this mean, then, in terms of where
you live and where I live? In how many of your relationships, think, in how many of your relationships, intimate,
primary, personal relationships, in which your power of
whatever character places another human being at your
mercy, are you so full of pride, arrogance, and personal insecurity as a human being that you dare not run the risk of
establishing within yourself voluntary distance between the
expression of your will on the life of another and where you
are located? Now, if you act that way, that is, if you establish
this distance, then at once you begin to participate in a dimension of living and experiencing, in a dimension of reality that lifts you into a category of an authentic child, son,
of God, for a principle now moves more and more to the
core of your being which says that you, as a person who
feels himself to be of infinite worth and significance in the
presence of God, recognizes, honors this quality in him by

dealing with your fellows out of the stirring vitality of this inner awareness of sanction.

Now one more little thing. Obviously, there are all sorts of fringes that cannot be touched this morning, but the principle is what I want us to grip, because then we can be working on it for days and days, and months, and years, for the rest of our lives. There is at the bottom, at the ground of all of the meaning of justice and mercy, what I think of as being a structure, the integrity of a moral order, and a moral order is one in which there is an inherent and inevitable relationship between the deed and the consequence. The degree to which I am willing to take my position on the moral integrity of life, to that degree I am willing to affirm in how I live from day to day that the evil deed does not go unpunished, but I am not the avenger; my responsibility is to keep alive this margin between the consequence of the exercise of the power which may be mine, an advantage which may be mine, and what I feel and sense as being what I want if the situation were reversed. I am merciful when I become in my simple, informal, or formal human relationships the kind of sensitive human being who makes this distance possible between the ruthless application of his will, his desire as it moves out toward another human being, and what he does. And in so doing, the strength of God becomes available to me in terms of insight, in terms of endurance, in terms of weakness of spirit, in terms of a benediction of his grace. Justice. Mercy. Mercy. Justice.

CLOSING PRAYER

There is all of the confusion inspired by our weakness and our inadequacy and our failure that we make as a part of the offering of our lives to thee, O God, our Father. What in us is dark, illumine. What is low, raise and support, to the end that in ways that we can understand, and in ways that transcend the limitations of our understanding, we may be living instruments in thy hands. Now, do not let us separate from thy spirit, as we separate one from the other, but go with us, O God; go with us, our Father.

15

CONCERNING PRAYER: PRAYER AND PRESSURE

The Unjust Judge (Luke 18:1-5)
and the Friend at Midnight (Luke 11:5-8)

In this sermon[1] Thurman reflects on two parables that at
first glance seem to make the same problematic point: we
should be persistently relentless at prayer.[2] Why is that
problematic? These two parables, especially the parable of
the unjust judge, seem to imply that God is reluctant to
help petitioners in desperate need and responds only to persistent pressure. Is God like a corrupt judge or an apparently unsympathetic neighbor? Of course not. Jesus is
instead artistically creating striking images and characters
to argue—as a rabbi might argue from the lesser to the
greater—that if human beings, "for all your evil you know

---

1. Previously published as "Prayer and Pressure" in Howard
Thurman, The Growing Edge (Richmond, IN: Friends United Press,
1974), 45–53. Published in this volume with permission granted by
Friends United Press.

2. One of Thurman's key resources for his study of the parables,
Buttrick's The Parables of Jesus, says that these "two stories are so strik-
ingly similar in purpose that they might almost be termed twin parables." George A. Buttrick, The Parables of Jesus (New York: Richard R.
Smith, 1930), 167. A few other aspects of Thurman's interpretation, such
as the widow following the judge home, seem to be dependent on Buttrick as well.

to give your children what is good, how much more will your Father give the holy Spirit from heaven to those who ask him!" (Luke 11:13). For example, Jesus asks, perhaps with a twinkle in his eye, if even a corrupt, unrighteous, and heartless judge will eventually give justice to an aggrieved widow will not God our loving father respond to God's children when they call out to God?[3]

The true focus of these prayers, Thurman argues, is on our attitudes concerning prayer. God does not need to be pressured; God is not lost in a state of indecision about how to respond to our prayers so that our persistence is necessary for God to render judgment and take action. Instead, Thurman insists that the true focus in these two parables is on us. He then cites the story of the paralyzed man who was healed by Jesus after an extraordinary effort by his friends to bring him, despite the crowds around Jesus, into Jesus's presence by digging through the roof of the house where Jesus was teaching (Luke 5:17-26). Thurman concludes that we do not need to put pressure on God. Instead, we need to put pressure on ourselves to become totally exposed to God, because it is our responsibility to ensure that our primary commitment, relationship, and loyalty are to God in everything we do in our daily lives. Our prayers, then, become the "creative synthesis" and expression of everything else we do at all times. Ultimately we have to trust that God, in God's infinite wisdom, will take action one way or another.

---

3. Thurman again demonstrates his familiarity with historical Jesus scholarship in his aside about our lack of certainty as far as recovering Jesus's original context and intention in these parables. Yet Thurman also captures, in our view, the authentic message of the historical Jesus in these reflections on Jesus's parables.

Concerning Prayer: Prayer and Pressure

Meditation

The peace of God,
    which passeth all understanding,
    shall guard my heart and thoughts.

There is the peace that comes
when lowering clouds burst
and the whole landscape is drenched in rain,
refreshing and cool.

There is the peace that comes
when hours of sleeplessness
are finally swallowed up in sleep,
deeply relaxing and calm.

There is a peace that comes
when what has lurked so long
in the shadow of my mind
stands out in the light.
I face it, call it by its name,
for better or for worse.

There is a peace that comes
when sorrow is not relieved,
when pain is not required,
when tragedy remains tragedy,
    stark and literal,
when failure continues through all the days
to be failure.

Is all this the peace of God?
Or is it the intimation of the peace of God?

The Peace of God
    shall guard my heart and thoughts.

There are feelings, untamed and unmanageable
        in my heart:
The bitterness of a great hatred, not yet absorbed;
    The moving light of love, unrequited or
            unfulfilled,
        casting its shafts down all corridors of my days;
        the unnamed anxiety brought on by nothing
            in particular,
        some strange foreboding of coming disaster
            that does not yet appear;
    The overwhelming hunger of God that
            underscores all the ambitions, dreams and
            restlessness of my churning spirit.

Hold them, O peace of God, until Thy perfect
    work is in them fulfilled.

The Peace of God, which passes all understanding,
    shall guard my heart and my thoughts.

Into God's keeping do I yield my heart and
        thoughts, yea, my life—
with its strength and weakness
its failure and success,
its shame and its purity.

O Peace of God, settle over me and within me
so that I cannot tell mine from thine
and thine from mine.

Prayer and pressure!

We are thinking of one of the very simple and natural expressions of the human spirit when it is exposed directly to the starkness, the intimate insistence of great need and tragedy. Prayer is for many of us the act of barnstorming the gates of heaven, wanting something for ourselves, desperately wanting something for someone else; turning to God in our extremity, as indeed we may, and are privileged to do. But always the point of reference is ourselves—our need for something that will relieve the pressure on us, for something that will make our lives easier, our way smoother, for something that will turn our darkness into light, that will lift the burden from our shoulders. Very often it seems as if we think of God as one who responds only to pressure that we exert upon him out of our necessity. Evidently, we think that God cannot make up his mind; that he is in a state of indecision until we remind him where we are in the universe and how great is our predicament. We call his attention to ourselves, and our needs, and our desperation. We even enlist the support of other people, that we may become an organized pressure group, to wrest from the stubborn and recalcitrant hands of an arbitrary God that which he is withholding.

Two stories from the lips of Jesus have been used again and again in this connection. They have been lifted, perhaps out of the meaning which he had in mind, but let me sketch these two stories that we may hold them before us.

One is a story of a judge who had no fear of man, no fear of God, no fear of fear. Apparently appointed for life, he was above the political process. A certain widow needed something desperately, something that this judge could give her. Every time he came to his outer chamber, there she was. When he would start home for his lunch, she

walked a respectful distance behind him, stating her case.
Everywhere he went, there she turned up, always saying the
same thing. "Will you do this for me?" And finally, he re-
lented and did it, not because he wanted to, not because he
cared for her predicament, not because of any far-flung or
intimate interpretation of the meaning of justice to which
he was committed as a jurist. No. He did what the woman
asked just because she kept worrying him, annoying him,
harassing him; in order that he might have peace, he gave
her peace.

The other story is that of a man who had unexpected
visitors late one night. They were overnight visitors, and
they were hungry. He didn't have any food to give them.
Jesus says [that] he didn't have any bread. But he remembered that his neighbor next door might have some bread
that he could borrow. He knocked at the door and the
neighbor asked, "Who is it?" He identified himself, saying,
"I didn't come for a social call, I want to borrow some
bread."

"But I can't get up; I don't know if I have any food; be-
sides I was just getting off to sleep after wrestling with in-
somnia for a long time. Now you come to disturb me. Go
on back home like a good neighbor." He drifted off to
sleep, but the knocking came again; he was called back
into consciousness. On and on that went, until finally he
got up. He gave bread to his neighbor, not because he
loved him, not because he cared anything about the hungry visitors. He gave the bread finally because he wanted to
go to sleep. Now the picture that comes to us is that God
is like that, that God has to be convinced, that he can be
convinced only if we give him no ease, until at last we bend
his will to meet our private demands. Pressure! Pressure!
Pressure!

I think this says something about God that is unworthy;
terribly unworthy! The point of the stories is not as is often

indicated that God must be subjected to pressure in order to act on our behalf.

There is another kind of pressure which I think is more relevant and nearer to the real meaning of prayer. This is the pressure that human need makes upon us, which often is so unrelieved and intense in its character that we dare not present ourselves to God without including it. You remember a story that Jesus tells in this connection. Here was a man bedridden. His friends were deeply identified with him in his suffering and his need. They heard that Jesus was in the village and believed that he would minister to extreme need. So they thought that if this bedridden man could be brought into a face-to-face, primary, intimate exposure to, and encounter with, the love of Jesus, then a miracle would take place. The problem was how to get these two together. They went to the house where Jesus was and the house was packed with people standing in all the entrances. The yard, too, was crowded. There seemed no way that they could call their friend's need to Jesus's attention. Then they noticed that the roof wasn't so very high. If they worked together on it, they might jockey their friend up to the roof. If they could tear away some of the thatched patches, they could let him down through the roof. All this they did and their friend was brought into direct contact with the love and vitality of Jesus.

The meaning? I respond to the pressure of human need with such utterness that I cannot separate myself from the need. Therefore, I can never lay bare my own soul to the life, to the love, to the scrutiny, to the wisdom, to the judgment of God, without including in it others' needs that keep pulling at me.

I remember visiting a certain women's college whose dean I had known for many years. In the afternoon, when I was at tea with her, I met her mother, who was a lady about ninety years old. After the dean had to leave to go to another meeting, the mother said to me, "I'm very glad that my daughter has left, because I want to talk to you about something. I listened to what you had to say this morning in chapel, and I want to tell you something. I have been a member of a certain church for more than fifty-five years. We have a minister at that church now whom we do not love very much. As a matter of fact, he is not able to lead us and should have left long ago. He knows that we feel he should go, but he says that the Spirit of God tells him to stay, despite all our efforts. About a week ago, I decided that I must do something about it. I took the entire afternoon off in my room. I began with the day I joined the church, more than a half-century ago, and unhurriedly, I reviewed my life in relation to the church, remembering all kinds of details, things that I hadn't thought of for years and years. I brought myself and the church up to the present moment and the present crisis. I went into detail, explaining to the Lord all about us, and about the minister, and then when I finished, I said, 'Now Lord, I have given you all the facts. Take them and do the best that you can. I have no suggestions to make.'"

Pressure should not be put upon God. The right place for pressure is upon me, upon you, to bring my life, your life, in its totality, to an exposure to God. Not to give God orders. Not to presume that we are omniscient and can always understand what is best for us—tempting and natural as this is. We must ingather the fragments of our lives, the concerns of our spirits, the loves of our hearts—all the aspects and dimensions of our living—we must ingather these and hold them in exposure to God. That is the ultimate responsibility of the human spirit. The Spirit of God, brooding over this stuff of our lives, will knead it and fashion it, infuse it with life, or withdraw vitality from some aspects of it. All of that is divine prerogative. Our obligation is to make the exposure.

Now, this we cannot do unless we practice the habit of focusing our lives, somewhat according to the principle of recollection emphasized in historical Catholicism. There must be a conscious awareness of God in the shadow of our minds, day by day, as we handle our affairs, perform our tasks, fulfill our duties. All that we do must be referred to this point of awareness within us. We are not pursuing something esoteric and aesthetic.

We are developing the habit of holding in mind that our primary relationship and our primary loyalty, our ultimate commitment, is to God. The radical result of the conversion of the human spirit to God is that there is this riding point of referral that is always present in the things that we do, in the decisions that we make. It is in some ways like the thing that happens when a person has some kind of disease that he has to watch. He knows that he is perfectly normal in many ways; but he must never forget, in all of the details of his living, whatever the nature of his excitement and joy and enthusiasm—he must never forget that his heart isn't quite so strong as it was. Any constant awareness moves gradually to the center of consciousness until it becomes one with consciousness; thus all that I do and think and feel and delight in ultimately stands or falls before the scrutiny, the judgment, and the love of God. Now if living moment to moment, day by day, as I go about my tasks and responsibilities, that is my pattern of behavior, then, when the time comes to enter the silent moment of prayer, there is merely a heightening of my experience. What I do in the moment of prayer is merely the creative synthesis of what I do always. And the pressure, the relentless pressure, is on me to live so that I desire to withhold nothing from [God]—to let his life and his love and his scrutiny play over the stuff of my days. And that is enough. What he does with it is not my affair.

BENEDICTION

O Love of God, Love of God, draw us in all the fragmenta-
tion of our splintered living, into the all-encompassing
grasp of thy Self. For us, this is enough. This is enough. Dismiss us with thy Spirit, as thou dost deal gently and tenderly
with all the limitations of our structure and our living that
we may not be alone in the way that we take, O God, our
Father.

CONCLUSION

Only so much do I know, as I have lived. Instantly we know whose words are loaded with life, and whose not.[1]

Just then a lawyer stood up to test Jesus. "Teacher," he said, "what must I do to inherit eternal life?" He said to him, "What is written in the law? What do you read there?" He answered, "You shall love the Lord your God with all your heart, and with all your soul, and with all your strength, and with all your mind; and your neighbour as yourself." And he said to him, "You have given the right answer; do this, and you will live." (Luke 10:25–28)

Simon Peter answered him, "Lord, to whom can we go? You have the words of eternal life." (John 6:68)

One can tell by the language people use, says Ralph Waldo Emerson, whether they are full of life or whether they are not. Howard Thurman's words, as the sermons in this volume demonstrate, are very often if not almost always "loaded with life." That is why, as Sue Bailey Thurman observed, Howard Thurman is indeed "a seeker and finder of

---

1. Ralph Waldo Emerson, "The American Scholar" in *Nature and Selected Essays* (New York: Penguin, 2003), 92.

genuine existence" and can be described as a "tutor to the world."[2]

We believe that Thurman's sermons on the parables of Jesus can provide fresh courage for another generation of conscientious citizens in the throes of social activism and in a moment when people can declare or reaffirm their binding commitment to the vision of the kingdom of God and the resulting human community proclaimed by Jesus in these parables and re-enacted in Thurman's sermons about them.

Thurman is not an expository preacher focusing intently on the text of scripture. His approach, as his mysticism leads him to do, is to connect with his congregation and to be "entirely devoted to the meaning and the experience of our common quest and journey."[3] This spirit—including the desire to encounter the Spirit—means that Thurman often does not preach from manuscripts or even notes; reading these sermon transcriptions gives only a hint of the way in which Thurman thinks through issues as he proceeds in the worship experience to encounter, along with his congregation, the Spirit of God, fundamental ideas of religious and human experience, and scripture. All of this occurs in the dialogic and communal experience of worship. Therefore, in addition to reading these sermons,

---

2. As described in the opening words in the introduction to this volume.

3. Howard Thurman, *With Head and Heart: The Autobiography of Howard Thurman* (New York: Harcourt Brace Jovanovich, 1979), 73. As Thurman writes in the preface to his collection of sermons, *The Growing Edge:* "For me the sermon is an act of worship in which the preacher exposes his mind and spirit as they seek to reveal the working of the spirit of the living God upon them. It is a searching moment! The atmosphere is one charged with the dynamics of worship and the surrender and commitment which worship inspires." Howard Thurman, *The Growing Edge* (Richmond, IN: Friends United Press, 1974), ix.

we encourage *readers* of Thurman to become avid *listeners* of Thurman.

Thurman's foreword in the collection of his sermons, *Temptations of Jesus*, offers key insights about his intentions as a preacher proclaiming the message of Jesus of Nazareth: "These are not five lectures. They are not five critical essays. They are five sermons, having as their fundamental purpose the illumination of the imagination, the stirring of the heart, and the challenge to live life meaningfully."[4] Thurman's sermons on the parables of Jesus serve a similar purpose: they offer clues for living in harmony with the will of God and the purpose of life.

Similarly, Thurman's interpretations of the parables of Jesus reveal interesting aspects of his approach to biblical interpretation and how the Bible should be applied in one's life. His sermons include observations about how parables work, how they are effective rhetorically by their use of particular words, images, or other aspects of their composition. Thurman admires, for example, the genius in Jesus's stories, the turn of phrase—such as the priest in the parable of the Good Samaritan "walking by the other side"—or the mysterious and curious absences—where is the mother, for example, in the parable of the Prodigal Son?

In addition, Thurman examines carefully what parables mean, the major points they make to their readers or hearers. This aspect, of course, derives from how parables of Jesus work: they excite the imagination and stimulate the mind (cf. chapter 1). Thurman recognizes the dialogic nature of Jesus's parables, and he delights in exploring the

---

4. Howard Thurman, *Temptations of Jesus* (Richmond, IN: Friends United Press, 1978), 5. In those sermons, Thurman then notes, "We see the Master as He struggled to find a way which will be for him the Way in which he can walk in utter harmony with the Will of his Father and the purpose of life. This too is what we seek, and in his answer we may find precious clues for ourselves."

possibilities inherent in these parables: not just how they say what they say, but what they have to say, what meanings we can mine from them. For Thurman, these explorations are communal, and he invites his audiences to travel with him on these expeditions, often expressing his own hesitation and asking his hearers over and over again in these sermons, "What do you think?" or "Do you believe that?" or "What do you think he is talking about?" or "What does all this mean?" or "What is [Jesus's] religion hammering at?"

But, most important, Thurman's sermons bring into particular focus what parables want. Parables are not merely stories to be enjoyed or morality tales with simple answers to guide our daily living. The parables of Jesus are stories that enable us to encounter God and, in the process, challenge us to adopt sometimes radically different views of God, ourselves, other human beings, the world, and how God works in the world. In the process of their telling and retelling, as we encounter God, Jesus's parables challenge us to respond. We are meant to be transformed, and this personal transformation causes us to act, to do things, not just to think things, challenging us to take action in our lives and in the world in concrete ways.[5]

We see constantly in these sermons Thurman's relentless pursuit of decision-making and the actions that proceed from those decisions. His question of "What do you think?" is a necessary prelude to the more important questions he poses, "How do you live it?"[6] or "So what do I do?" or "Will you try it and see?" or "Are you willing to try that? Are you willing to try it really? To work at it?"[7]

---

5. David B. Gowler, *The Parables after Jesus* (Grand Rapids, MI: Baker Academic, 2017), 255–57.

6. See, for example, Thurman's conclusion in the sermon in chapter 1.

7. See, for example, Thurman's sermon in chapter 5.

Perhaps these questions and challenges posed by Thurman are his way of echoing if not re-enacting the questions and challenges of the person in whose footsteps he attempts to walk: Jesus of Nazareth, who after telling the parable of the Good Samaritan instructs the lawyer, and everyone with ears to hear, to "go and do likewise" (Luke 10:37). Or, as Thurman puts it:

> Do not shrink, then, from that which turns up in your road, suddenly making of you an ultimate demand. Know that if you respond with all that you have, your little life takes on a meaning in the light of which even death itself is a little thing. To miss it because of fear, timidity, pride, arrogance, self-righteousness, deceit, to miss it is to wander down your road in darkness, and what a darkness, what a darkness it is for you.

> Go thy way, all things say. Thou hast thy way to go. Thou hast thy time to live. Do thy thing. Know thou this that there is no other who can do for thee that which is appointed thee of God. So go thy way and do thy thing. (chapter 11)